I (was) Volunteered to Chair the Auction.

HELP!

RUTH MCCURDY
AND
LINDA OPPENHEIM

StoryMaster Press
Houston, Texas

Published in The United States of America by
StoryMaster Press
14520 Memorial Drive
Suite M – 141
Houston, Texas 77079

Editor: Steve McCurdy

Library of Congress Control Number: 2004096808

International Standard Book Number (ISBN): 0-9761-1790-8

Printed in the United States of America
First Edition 2004

Cover Design and Layout
SMC Design
14631 Kimberley
Houston, Texas

First Edition 2004

StoryMaster Press books are available for bulk discount. Contact us for special pricing throuth www.storymasterpress.com/auctionhelp

Our Thanks-

We want to express our very special thanks to folks who read through drafts and notes and gave us some of their valuable time to answer our questions and share great insights for the book – Karen McCarver, Cathy McDonell, Caren Steffes, and Amy Meyers.

And Dedications-

I dedicate this book to my husband, Roger. He understands me, and knows me, and he still loves me. I feel it from him daily, even when I am cranky and in the throws of a volunteering nightmare. He makes me feel that what ever I undertake I will be successful. He laughs with me and shares my everyday. He breathes in and I breathe out - we are a team. For this I am grateful. He gives me the strength to be who I am. With the ever-changing seasons of our life we move together and stay as one. His support is undying and my love for him has no end.

I also want to dedicate the book to my children, without whom I would not have recognized the potential in myself. A day never ends without my being in awe that they are mine. Lastly to Ruth and Steve McCurdy. They plucked this pick-a-little lady out of the crowd and saw something in me that I had not. But that is what makes them so special; they see what others cannot. They mold and shape people and never really know the impact of whom they have touched. I thank them for all the lessons learned and all the lessons to come.

Linda Oppenheim

When thinking about writing a dedication – I wondered how many people would actually spend time reading it. Then I realized that the most important aspect of writing a book dedication is the opportunity to honor the people in your life who believe in you and help you to achieve something that is very important to you.

To my husband, Steve, thank you for spending endless hours listening to our ideas, reading and editing our words and making the book seem more like a visit with friends than a cookbook. Most importantly, thanks for loving me, being my best friend, and for the hours of laughter that we share.

To my children, Ashlee, Chase, and Chelsea – You brighten my life and bring me endless joy! Without you guys I wouldn't've had the opportunity to make the zany journey of a volunteer.

To my co-author, Linda – Thank you for your endless energy, your unwavering enthusiasm, your wild sense of humor and your willingness to do anything to support a friend.

And finally, to my mother – Thank you for raising me with the belief that I could do anything that I decided to do.

As Linda would say... Who knew?

Ruth McCurdy

Table of Contents

Introduction

What's This Auction Thing All About?

We were standing in the International Terminal waiting for them to clear customs. We could see from the monitors that the plane had been on the ground for a while...

The doors opened and they came dragging out. Tired, worn, schlepping luggage much too big for them... and different. They were different. They were world travelers who had seen another country, tried (some of them) different foods, experienced things I didn't get to see until I was grown. They were tired but they glowed with that air that only a real experience can give a kid. They were changed...

That was when I realized it was worth it. Perhaps I'd realized it before, but seeing them walk back through that gate convinced me at the deepest levels that all the fear and fun and exhilaration and disappointment and anticipation and committee meetings and problem solving and late night phone calls and last minute adjustments and hair appointments and pick-ups and deliveries... all of it was worth it. We had raised the money – sent the kids – and had changed lives. They would never be the same.

This book is dedicated to those of you who are at the FRONT END of that process. You just got the job and aren't sure where to start. Just as you cannot convincingly reassure your children that their vegetables are good for them we cannot reassure you that the journey you are on will pay rewards... but it has for us – and thousands like us. So we think it will be true for you also.

In this book we will map out everything you need to do to get from point zero (total ignorance)—to successful completion (elegant master of chair-ship). There are a LOT of steps. But each one is just a step. It isn't brain surgery. Almost any volunteer you recruit can fulfill 80% of the jobs we will describe and we'll help you identify the key players for that other critical 20%.

In "Hello Dolly" Dolly Levi says, "...doing those four or five things that make life worth living takes a little money. Not a lot... but some."

Well, Dolly was right. It does take some money... and sometimes it even takes A LOT!! Raising funds is ALWAYS a problem for schools, churches, alumni organizations... everyone.

A popular and enormously successful method is the GALA EVENT featuring a Live and/or Silent Auction. They are popular because the concept is dirt simple. Now, it sounds simple on the surface. Just find businesses that care about the community or their perception in the community to donate things to sell. Then get people who love your organization to come buy those things that they want and might have bought anyway – and maybe save a little money in the process. Everyone wins; the merchants, the buyers, and the beneficiaries of the organization.

Like we said... sounds simple. Here's another simple concept – marriage. Find someone you like, join up and share a life together. If you have ever chaired an auction or gotten married you know that neither are as simple to do as they are to understand. In fact, if we knew what we were getting into – some of us might not do it at all. For others of us, though, even knowing the price wouldn't stop us 'cuz we know the payoff is worth it. Somewhat like marriage, so many auction fundraisers are done a year that it seems like they would be automatic. They aren't. They take work.

Someone has to:
- decide on the amount to be raised (or aimed for)
- come up with a theme
- find a location
- select a menu
- get folks to contribute things to auction off
- go get those things
- store those things somewhere
- track those things
- get them to the venue to be auctioned
- display them attractively and describe them
- find a way to take bids
- advertise, market, beg and plead to get people to come to the event
- decorate everything in accordance with the theme... for 39¢
- print a program so folks know what to expect

- make a catalogue of all the stuff up for bid
- set up the live auction
- find an auctioneer who get people to buy and pay more
- set up the silent auction
- create a system so people can bid and you can find them
- get people to gladly pay to come and then pay to buy things
- figure out who bought what and for how much
- collect the money
- deliver the stuff
- clean up the venue
- thank the donors and the buyers so they'll do it again
- thank your team so they will do it again
- thank your family so you can come home
- thank your therapist for keeping you sane – or at least alive!!

In marriage we often spend quite a while trying to figure out who is supposed to do what job. Particularly when there are disputes over who is ACTUALLY in charge. Drafting help can be a problem, too. But the auction process is MUCH easier to pull off and define. In the following pages we'll help you detail EVERY job that needs to be done, define WHEN each job must be completed, specify what FINISHED looks like for each task, and we'll hold your hand as you track it all, and even describe in detail how to recruit and manage others so that they will gladly help out.

We'll also direct you to our website for free documents, reports, and other tools to help you through the process. If we've left anything out we'll even give you our email address so you can ask us directly.

We're here to help, because… when you do this right it is:

- fun,
- manageable,
- and, makes a difference in lives.

And we believe that is absolutely… WORTH IT!

Ruth McCurdy
Linda Oppenheim

*The Basic Things
to Know and Do*

Chapter 1

When do I do what???

The Event Timeline

As you begin gathering your thoughts about your upcoming event, its best to take a 60,000 foot view of all the tasks that need to be done and formulate a timeline that details when each task needs to be done. If this is your first time to chair an event like this, we recommend that you give yourself a little extra time to get things done.

Your timeline will vary somewhat based upon the nature of your event. One extreme is the gala that is extremely elegant with many intricate components involved and may require over a year in the planning. At the opposite extreme are the more casual, easier-to-implement plans that may take much less time. Sometimes the date on which you need to book the venue will drive the start date of your timeline. We know of one example where the Event Chairperson was named 11 months prior to the event and the committees formed and began working 10 months prior to the event. To help you get started, we created a timeline beginning at 6 months prior to an event. Reviewing this timeline will give you a good idea of all of the tasks that need to be done to ensure that your event is a success.

We recommend that you prepare an event calendar, highlight specific deadlines, and provide a copy to all of your committee chairpersons. Automated tools such as Microsoft Outlook and Palm Pilots are very helpful as you calendar your event because they have features that will remind you when certain activities are due.

SUCCESSS TIP: Though it may be a bit more time consuming it is important that you check the calendars of other organizations with which your members are affiliated. We'll never forget the live/silent auction event that was scheduled the same weekend as an All-Church Women's Retreat. Who knew? In this case it was the retreat that was rescheduled late in the game in order to accommodate a speaker. It was much too late for us to move our event. As it was, fewer women attended the auction than we had hoped and women in our group who wanted to go on the retreat had to stay to manage a less than successful event. It ended up being a lose-lose result with bad feelings all around – but very difficult to avoid.

Six months prior to the event

- chairperson designated
- set the date & time – be sure to check the organization's calendar for a time that will not conflict with a lot of other events
- book the venue, the menu, and draft a design of the event's floor plan for the event
- appoint committee chairpersons
- event chairperson holds first meeting with committee chairpersons
- chairpersons determine number of volunteers needed
- select the theme
- design the logo and place on all correspondence
- create the volunteer recruiting plan
- design flyers & begin recruiting
- identify auctioneer candidates
- secure tax exempt number for the organization and distribute to committee chairpersons via a letter or form
- print all donation forms in triplicate (one copy for donor, one copy for auction chair and one copy stays with the item)
- investigate entertainment options
- set up the auction data base

Five months prior to the event
- event chairperson holds first committee meeting (include all volunteers)
- committee chairpersons submit budgets
- finalize the master budget
- treasurer writes reimbursement policy and gives copies to committee chairpersons
- establish advertising space sizes and pricing
- begin soliciting for advertisers, underwriters and auction item donors
- distribute a volunteer directory organized by committee to all participants
- begin publicity with a "save the date theme"
- book the auctioneer
- identify group project leaders and begin planning group projects (if applicable)
- secure entertainment

Four months prior to the event
- develop the decorations plan
- begin cataloging donations (or as soon as you start to receive them)
- send thank-you notes for all donations to date
- publicize the event
- chairperson recognizes volunteers
- determine how payment is accepted for reservations and for auction items
- prepare the invitation mailing list

Three months prior to the event
- design invitations & program cover
- create a list of all group projects that will be auctioned
- publicize the event
- catalog donations

Two months prior to the event

- print invitations and program cover
- publicize the event
- begin collecting material for decorations
- catalogue donations

One month prior to the event

- begin publicizing the types of auction items received to date
- mail invitations
- all ads are in and underwriters noted
- chairperson recognizes volunteers
- catalogue donations

Three weeks prior to the event

- collect all completed group projects
- update list of auction items for publicity
- arrange to pick up silent auction items
- create bid sheets for silent auction
- create description sheets for silent auction
- determine payment options for auction items sold
- catalogue donations

Two weeks prior to the event

- update list of auction items for publicity
- begin organizing the silent auction items in storage
- collect props for displaying auction donation items
- finalize the floor plan for the dinner, entertainment, and auction areas
- secure auction paddles for live auction
- catalogue donations

One week prior to the event
- update list of auction items for publicity
- prepare silent auction envelopes for check out
- prepare gift certificates as needed
- prepare list of attendees and prepare name tags if needed
- prepare check-in packets for guests
- prepare a list of all auction items for checkout
- catalogue donations

Day of the event
- give script to auctioneer
- transport all auction items to venue
- test the sound system very early (then don't change it)
- set up silent auction
- set up checkout area - if a credit card machine is to be used – test it

Evening of the event
- relax – you deserve it!
- transport remaining items from auction to pre-arranged pick-up site

One week after the event
- finalize any thank-you notes to donors
- complete treasurer's report
- prepare & distribute the final publicity regarding the results
- all committee chairpersons complete notebook entries

Two weeks after the event
- chairperson finalizes the notebook
- collapse

Use this timeline as a springboard for your ideas. To download a free timeline worksheet go to www.storymasterpress.com/auctionhelp and develop one that best suits the activities associated with your event.

Chapter 2

Where will this party be, and what's for dinner?
(... and just know that I'm not cooking!)

Selecting the Venue and Menu

As the Event Chairperson, selecting the venue is one of the first and most important activities that you will do as you begin your planning. The selection of the venue dictates the following:

- whether the event is casual or formal

- the location and flow of the silent auction, dining, and live auction areas

- the type of decorations that you will be able to use

- menu choices

- serving options - buffet or seated dinner

- the number of attendees

- the event activities

In some instances, the availability of the venue may also dictate the date of the event. Check with your group's calendar when finalizing the date to determine any conflicts that would cause people to have to choose between events. The selection process should be thorough and given a lot of thought, and not just by YOU! You want to put a LOT of minds on this one! (Remember the auction vs. retreat fiasco!!)

How to Begin

There are several things to consider as you begin the selection process. First, if the event has been held previously, review each of the previous venues and any notes about them to determine the pros and cons of each. Next, create a list of known requirements for the event. Here are some questions to help guide your thinking:

1. What special activities will be taking place during the event? For example, will there be dancing requiring a dance floor or entertainment that requires a stage, piano, sound system, special lighting?

2. Do you want to serve a meal or hors d'oevres? How do you want the meal served – buffet style or a seated dinner?

3. What is the maximum that we want to charge for a ticket? The answer to this question is critical because the costs associated with some venues may be significantly higher than others.

4. Will alcohol be served? If so, do we want to add the cost of two drinks to each ticket to the event and provide the guests drink tickets? Or, do we have a cash bar – and if so, who will man it?

5. Do we want parking included in the package? If so, do we want valet parking or is it acceptable or preferable to have guests park their own cars?

6. What areas of town are suitable for the event? How far are your guests willing to drive?

7. What time does the event begin and end?

Contacting Venues

Once you've narrowed down your ideas using these questions, it's time to list the questions that you want answered about the venue. We recommend that you write them down so that when you begin to interview prospective venues, you'll have them available and you are less likely to forget them. When you contact the venue, ask to speak to someone in the sales and catering department.

Here are some questions that we recommend:

1. Have they hosted an event like this before? If so, what recommendations do they have? If they have hosted an event like yours, they will have a good idea about the set up and what works best in their venue.

2. Based upon the time of day that you want to hold your event, what menu choices are available for a buffet? A seated meal? What are the costs of each? Can you get a copy of the menu choices? Are menu substitutions allowed?

3. What kind of deposit is required?

4. What is the date on which you need to provide them a final count of attendees?

5. What audio/visual equipment is available and is it part of the cost of the room?

6. What is the availability of the venue staff prior to and the day of the event?

7. How many servers are included in the price per person?

8. If alcoholic drinks are served, how many cash bars should you have and where should they be located?

9. Is there a charge for a bartender? Is the bartender responsible for selling the drink tickets or do have our volunteers do it? (We recommend that the bartender do it – it is so much easier and THEY make that revenue… not us. However, in some venues the organization is REQUIRED to sell the tickets to reduce the liability borne by the venue)

10.   How early can you have access to the silent auction, live auction and dining area on the day of the event? What time will the staff have the tables covered with cloths in the silent auction area? PUSH for as early as you can. Hair and nails take TIME!!!

11. What are the size and shapes of available tables?

12. What colors are available in the table linens? You may have an interest in color coordinating table linens with your theme and decorations.

13. Are their any restrictions relating to the type of decorations that are used?

14. Will the venue supply soft drinks, iced tea and water or maybe even lunch to the workers the day of the event? Everything is available at a price, but negotiate. We're bringing them business. Press a little for freebies wherever you can. Often just asking will do it.

15.   Are electrical outlets available in the silent auction rooms? Some of your display and prop items may need "juice!"

16.   Is the venue willing to make a donation for the live or silent auction? Don't forget this question! Most of the time the answer is "yes" and you'll have your first donated item!!! NOTE: Ruth's oldest daughter sold a LOT of Girl Scout cookies by calling friends and saying, "I'm selling Girl Scout Cookies… HOW MANY BOXES DO YOU WANT?" It never dawned on Ashlee that the person WOULDN'T buy her cookies. Let's learn from this natural saleswoman. If you ask, "WHAT is the venue willing to donate…" they will start thinking of how to answer that question positively.   If you ask "Will you?" the old "policy" answer is right in their pocket. The same technique applies when asking local businesses to support your cause. "What can you do?" produces much more fruit than, "Will you?" In the case of a venue, a meal for two or an overnight stay costs them almost nothing and provides them an inexpensive way to buy some good will and publicity. Also, asking this question BEFORE the deal is signed is a tad more powerful than after they have your deposit in their bank!

Visiting Venues

Once you've narrowed your list down further, the next step is to go see the venue and meet their staff. Even if you have attended an event at the venue previously, we recommend that go back with the requirements of your event in mind. There are several key objectives that you want to accomplish during your visit.

First, you want to make sure that the venue will accommodate your event comfortably. There may be several options presented to you regarding the staging of your event within the venue. For example, the venue may have a ballroom that is large enough to accommodate all of the activities of the event. You may also choose, if available, to have your meal and live auction in one room and a separate room or rooms, for the silent auction. Don't envision how it might be. WALK IT. Walk through each option to make sure that the flow will work for you.

Your second objective is to get a feel for the type of service that you can expect from the staff. Ask to meet some of them. In many instances, the sales department rep is the only person you meet - and they are paid to "sell" you on choosing their venue. When you meet someone on the staff, you may ask them if they have any suggestions for you regarding the success of your event. This will provide a chance for a conversation and may give you some really good ideas!

Your third objective is to establish a rapport with the individual with whom you will be working such as the sales person, catering manager, etc. This person will be very important to you as you move forward.

Finally, look for things to help you get folks excited about the venue. For example, it may be a country club and the room has a gorgeous view of a fountain that will be lit during the evening of the event. (Ask to come back during the actual hours of your event to see how it looks at night). There may be a bridge with a beautiful back drop of foliage that is perfect for picture taking! You may even want to take some digital pictures and email them to folks to get them jazzed about the venue. It never hurts to start creating a buzz about the event early in the game.

Finalizing the Venue

After the venue decision is made, your next step is to provide the venue with a floor plan that you would like to have set up for your event. This step allows the venue a chance to make certain that they can accommodate everything that you need.

Now you are ready to complete the contract with the venue. This step must not be taken lightly. Typically, the venue will create the contract and send it to you for review and your signature. As you review it, make sure that everything you have requested is listed so that there are no questions regarding your requirements. If you see something that is missing, ask that it be included *even if it seems trivial.*

Once you are ready to sign the contract, you'll need to prepare the deposit and include it with the signed documents. This guarantees that the venue has been booked and you are ready to go!

Happy hunting!!!

Chapter 3

How am I going to track all of this???

The Auction

One of the first steps in your event timeline (6 months prior to the event) is to create your auction database. The purpose of a database is to capture all of critical information associated with your event such as donors, donated items, invitations mailings lists, etc. Though a database can be manual, we highly recommend that you consider automation. An automated database can be updated quickly and it can be shared easily with all of your committee members.

Throughout this book, you will be introduced to forms and spreadsheets that you can use with off-the-shelf software like MS Word and Excel. Free copies of tools are also available to download from our website at www.storymasterpress.com/auctionhelp. Once downloaded, you can customize them to your needs very easily. Be aware, though, that the Excel forms often have formulae built right into them to run your calculations for you. Simply substituting your names and item identifications will give you a document ready to produce calculated reports at the click of a mouse.

Great silent auction events, regardless of size, formality or amenities, share a common reason for their success: organized, thoughtful planning that leverages, to the maximum extent possible, all of the resources that can be made available to the organization.

To fully achieve those benefits, savvy organizations select one of several software packages to assist in the preparation and event management process. This approach eliminates the need for manual records, helps produce many of the critical event materials, and facilitates both the check-in and the checkout processes.

Let's stop right here and head off the thousands of "we can't afford that" objections that may be rising. If this is your very first event you may think it makes more sense to try it manually and then, if it looks like this is the kind of fund raiser you will want to continue with THEN you'll consider automation. Ok. We see your point. What we KNOW is that a well run and well attended live/silent auction event raises money. Potentially LOTS of money. If you focus on GETTING GREAT ITEMS and GETTING PEOPLE THERE the automation can take almost ALL of the other burdens off of your shoulders.

"But the COST!!!" Right. It isn't free. So we always suggest that an organization find an underwriter to buy them the software and give them credit EVERY YEAR. Annual updates are usually quite reasonably priced and can be funded from the operating budget. As trite as it sounds you truly do have to, "Spend money to make money." Only in the dictionary does DIVIDEND come before INVESTMENT.

Silent Auction Events (or similar events, such as "Casino" events) have unique technology requirements that differ from those of other special events. First and foremost, the organization is SELLING something and collecting some form of PAYMENT at the event itself. Make it *easy* for the guests to DONATE money, and provide them with a professional receipt that can serve as a tax document as well as a formal thank-you note! The software supports that for you.

Other basic requirements revolve around the attributes of donated items, such as item categories, descriptions, values and so on. A small private school characterized their earlier event preparation as 'well intentioned, but inefficient.'

Their chairwoman told us, "We would use one volunteer to produce item display signs, another to produce a printed item catalog, a third to design item certificates, and a fourth to develop bid sheets. Coordination was a nightmare and we'd have re-work to do and a few embarrassing mistakes. Now we type the information [once] into a specialized database, and all of the materials we need are beautifully formatted and printed via the software."

Technology decisions depend upon each organization's particular goals, needs, and criteria. An implementation plan is then based on the specific software and/or services chosen.

In working with a variety of organizations, their leaders have told us horror stories of manual processes that didn't get the job done and of technology solutions that, though helpful, didn't provide everything they needed. The consensus among these veterans seems to be, "...buy all the flexibility that you can afford, because you will not think of everything you need up-front. It was imperative for us to select a vendor with a track record who could also offer at-the-event services and tailor those services to our needs."

With proper use of technology you can eliminate many manual tasks, avoid dozens of common errors, and save volunteers countless hours in the event preparation phase.

There are many software packages on the market, and they can all do the job to a varying degree of perfection. Our research indicates that the AuctionStar® package stands out, partly because it uses state-of-the-art technology in a unique way.

Why AuctionStar®?

We happen to know (and love) the AuctionStar® package, and will use that as an example throughout. Now, we know that one size doesn't fit all, and you may have good reasons for making a different choice. Nevertheless, here is a short introduction.

AuctionStar® is a special-purpose software system using a patented (U.S. Patent No. 5,803,500) bar code technology to speed up and intensify silent auction bidding. (DON'T let bar coding scare you… it is SO simple).

Guests sign-in and are provided with plenty of bar coded stickers that identify THEM. To bid they place one of their bar code stickers on the bid sheets next to pre-printed bid prices corresponding to their bid, e.g., $100, $125, $150, etc.

Sales are tallied up at the end using inexpensive or rented bar code scanners that identify the bidder and the final bid! CLICK!!! We consider the checkout system to be unsurpassed in efficiency and user friendliness.

Many nonprofit organizations select AuctionStar® because it enables a smooth check-in and fast checkout—two things that really affect the bottom line. Treating guests to an event as pleasurable as possible is a top priority—happy guests will come back next year and spend more!

The AuctionStar® software is also recognized as a tool to analyze purchase statistics: Who is bidding? Who is spending? What kinds of items are popular? What are the trends? All this information can be consolidated for future committee members.

Like so many great products in existence today, AuctionStar® was born out of dire need. Dr. Bjorn Mossberg developed the AuctionStar® software system after having received a distress call from his son's school. "Can't we make this SIMPLER some how????" The response from the school, and later the community, was extremely positive, and today virtually every type of nonprofit organization uses the package. Since 1996, CrestWare Inc. has provided software, services and equipment rental for events that include silent auction, casino, or other "collect-at-the-event" fundraisers.

The system has been developed based on the needs of actual nonprofit organizations, and the software has evolved to the point that it can handle virtually any situation that comes up during an event. This is a direct result of the company's practice of actually providing both supervising personnel and on-call telephone operators to a large number of events. Since they are "on-site with you" in so many ways, they TRULY understand the problems to be solved.

Selecting a Software Package

To properly assess an event software package you must start looking months before the event. Once selected, the evaluation of the software must then continue throughout the event night, and well into the planning for the next event. Should the package come up short, it's better to cut your losses and get something better for the next event— the cost will be more than recovered through improved functionality. By the same token, even if you currently are committed to another software package, it might still be useful to consider the different issues brought up in this chapter.

One of the main points with using a specialized auction software package is that data can be kept in a single place. This eliminates the need to enter the name of a guest, for instance, in two (or more) different places. Everything you need printed for the event should, of course, be printable by that package. Event material you need may include item display signs, item labels, bid sheets, an auction catalog (program), guest envelope labels, name tags, bid stickers, live auction bid paddles, underwriting letters, thank-you letters, guest lists, table lists, alphabetic queue signs (A-F, G-H, etc.) for check-in and checkout, invoices, and last, but not least, an abundance of final reports summarizing the results of your efforts.

During the data entry phase before the event, you want to be able to do "everything", for instance:

- import data from last year's auction, or perhaps from another software package, including a spreadsheet;

- keep track of special sections such as Live Auction and Big Board, plus Silent Auction with subcategories;

- package items, using supporting features such as listings and package dissolving;

- re-number and otherwise rearrange items, and move them around between item categories;

- automatically set minimum bids and raises based on some simple criterion, while maintaining the flexibility to modify special items on a case-by-case basis;

- track (enter and report on) ticket sales and underwriting, and handle pre-event sales;

- print mailing lists and mailing labels, plus all event materials (see partial list earlier);

- handle table assignments including quick, last minute, inevitable musical chairs.

Another reason for using a specialized package is to enable the smooth and proper handling of special requests—those that always materialize when everyone wants to check out at the same time.

Some non-standard situations that can come up during checkout are:

- The Johnson family won an item for $4,000, but now another family wants to kick in $1,000, leaving only $3,000 for the Johnson family to pay. As a result, the fair market value on the receipt/invoice must be changed.

- A donor is impressed by how much money her item fetched, and decides to double up, adding another identical item. When this occurs, a new bid sheet needs to be added along with a new item number. Ten seconds with software, 10 minutes (or impossible if on-site) manually.

- 30 minutes before silent auction closing the committee decides to slash prices by 50 percent on 17 items that have not yet fetched any bids. New bid sheets must be swiftly produced. VERY difficult without software.

- A party with 20 seats (a sign-up item) sold out, and the host is not available to clear expanding the guest list, so a wait-list needs to be created.

Now, while these "unplanned" scenarios may not occur during your event, our experience says SOMETHING LIKE IT WILL. You need to be prepared. Software can easily facilitate last minute changes.

Here are some other helpful tips to consider when shopping for software.

- Buy the most flexibility that you can afford. In general, you get what you pay for, and a cheap package typically is unsatisfactory even for a small event.
- Consider the support of your needs during and after the event, and don't focus solely on the preparation phase;
- Consider the intrinsic value of happy event guests and volunteers. How you treat these supporters now will determine your success in subsequent years.
- Will you be able to track sponsors, donors, table sales, and items donated during the event preparation stage?
- Does the software provide documentation to get started and plan for an event?
- How does the event night flow with the software? Are guests going to be waiting in line at check in or check out? Will you be able to know the auction results as soon as the invoices start coming out?
- Will you get statistical reports, necessary to give planners a framework to analyze their event, but also prepare for the next event?

Use these tips as guidelines for narrowing your search. And, before you purchase, ask for references and contact them.

Database Development

Once you've purchased your software, you will probably need at least two computer literate individuals, either paid staff or volunteers. One can do the data entry and event material printing, while the other person can handle automatic mailings, troubleshooting, and other non-routine tasks. Decide how to use the software system, and streamline your preparation process.

Listed below are the areas that you will track in your database. Specific details about each of these areas are discussed in subsequent chapters.

Donor Solicitation: Data from prior events should be used to send out solicitation letters, most commonly via simple export and mail merge procedures. Do not lose those important donors from one event to the next!

Underwriting: Use the tracking system for table sponsorships and major underwriters.

Invitations: Guest invitations typically are sent out about four to six weeks before the event. Use your software to produce mailing labels.

Reservations: Keep track of names, addresses and phone numbers, and any special needs that a guest might have (kosher, wheelchair bound, etc.). Table assignments are of course basic, and must be flexible and easy to use. Track ticket sales so that you can monitor along the way.

Donors and Donated Auction Items: Track each donor and the item donated. This information will be used for following events and thank you notes. If you choose to use AuctionStar®, item description sheets can be created from this information.

Bid Sheets: A bid sheet for each item will be developed in your database. If you choose to use AuctionStar® the bid sheet process takes on a whole new look.

AuctionStar® provides a patented bar code technology which encodes bidders, items, and prices with unique bar codes. Each bid sheet features identifying text plus a number of pre-printed bid options, the prices of which cannot be changed by the guest. Each bid option is represented by a dollar amounts plus a box for a bid sticker to be affixed by a bidding guests.

To sell an item you need to connect the three entities:

- which bidder (the last sticker) bought
- which item (top of bid sheet) for
- what price (next to bid sticker)?

If you can do that with three (or fewer) quick scans with a grocery store type bar code scanner, imagine what that will do for the speed and accuracy of your tallying-up phase! You have to see it to believe it!

Included in this book is a CD-Rom entitled AuctionStar® Demo along with instructions on how to review it. If you have an interest purchasing software, this demo will give you a great overview of the functionality and reporting capabilities that are available. Review the software options that are available in the market. Pick the one that is best for you.

For a link to AuctionStar® go to our website at:
www.storymasterpress.com/auctionhelp

Tell them you heard about them from the book!!

Chapter 4

Hi. Could you do a *LITTLE BITTY* job for me?

Volunteer Management

The success of your event sits squarely on the shoulders of your volunteers; however, very little time is usually given to thoughtful planning and management of these folks. This chapter is focused on the elements of designing and managing a successful volunteer program.

Planning

Careful planning is the first step in the design of a volunteer program that can ultimately manage itself. Give your best thought to what you need volunteers to do. Be as specific as possible. A detailed example is on the next page.

Your goal is to create an enthusiastic, motivated and CONFIDENT team of people who know exactly what is expected of them, and who are willing and capable of moving forward with their individual responsibilities and accomplishing their goals.

The best way to achieve this type of clarity is to develop a list of jobs that need to be done and the activities associated with each and clearly communicating that information to EVERYONE who needs to know. We're all human with a million pressures on us and a hunger to be a part of something successful. This is definitely an example of knowledge-is-power. Knowing WHAT to do, and HOW to do it is 98% of the mountain. The other 2% is getting started. Job descriptions sound dull as dishwater but they are a simple way to make a clean list that anyone can understand and click through.

A simple job description format that includes the title and purpose of the position, the activities and responsibilities associated with the position, and the approximate time commitment for each is the foundation upon which you can build any other information you find useful.

In our next chapter we will give you a big head start on what is arguably the most important task you can achieve! Detailed there are thorough breakdowns of all of the customary jobs. They are even logically broken down into bite-sized tasks. Every event, though, will have its own unique twists. So, your job is to make sure everyone else knows what their job is… on THIS project.   Here's a snapshot of one of them.

Volunteer Job Description

Position Title	Decorations Chairperson
Purpose of the position	Responsible for all decorations relating to the event
Activities	<ul><li>work with Event Chairperson on theme</li><li>work with Treasurer and Event Chairperson to determine the budget</li><li>design decorations for the dining tables, the entrance, the auction locations</li><li>gather all materials for the decorations</li><li>enlist volunteers for the committee</li><li>provide decorations for any activities prior to the event as needed</li><li>determine price of decorations if they are to be sold or raffled after the event</li><li>decorate the day of the event</li><li>collect any remaining decorations at the end of the event</li><li>provide Treasurer with receipts for all expenses incurred</li><li>write notes for the Event Notebook and give to the Event Chairperson</li></ul>
Approximate time commitment	2 - 3 hours a week prior to the event and 4 – 5 hours the day of the event. This will vary based upon the complexity of the decorations.

There are several advantages to committing the job assignment to paper.

- First, the process of writing the job description will ensure that you are capturing all of the pertinent details.

- Second, the job description provides the volunteer with a personal guide to accomplishing what is expected. This alone can prevent misunderstandings and potential unpleasantness down the line.

- Third, it can be a phenomenal recruiting tool. Having the job specifically defined – and thereby LIMITED – leaves room for a person to say "Yes. I can do that."

- Fourth, it is a simple accountability tool. "How are we doing on bullet 3?" is an easy and non-confrontational way to jog the elbow of a volunteer you fear may be a bit behind. They have had the job description in hand… they have agreed to do the job. Reporting on status can prompt YOUR bullet to go on THEIR today's to-do's.

- And finally, a record can be placed in an Event Notebook that can be used in subsequent years. Remember, we want to improve upon the wheel from year-to-year, not reinvent it from scratch!

Recruiting Volunteers

Once you have the job descriptions documented, the next step is to begin recruiting volunteers. A parent with even one child who is involved in multiple activities gets bombarded from all sides to come help and support. Multiply that by a kid or two and it is easy to see why there is more competition for volunteers than ever before. This also increases the number of EVENTS people have to decide between attending. Smart recruiting can help to solve BOTH problems.

Karen McCarver, a successful event Chairperson in Houston, Texas says it is vital to— "Include as many people in the process as possible – the more people that have a job, even a small one, the greater the likelihood they will be attending the event."

Look to everyone that has both direct and indirect involvement with your organization. For example, if you are doing a school auction, look to the parents, older siblings, and extended family members as possible volunteers. Even alums!!

There are three things to consider when recruiting volunteers.

- First, what recruiting tools and materials will you be using?
- Second, who will you recruit?
- Finally, how will you go about recruiting?

Recruiting Materials

Printed materials that are eye-catching and that indicate specific needs work best when trying to get the word out. Brightly colored paper that **"STANDS OUT"** gets noticed and read –which is exactly what you want to have happen. In addition to bright colors, unique shapes attract attention.

Here are a few great ideas:

- Trace around a hand and use –

   "We need some helping hands!"

- A circular shape is great with the message –

   "It's time to get a 'round' to being a volunteer!"

- Use a question mark with the message –

   "Ask what you can do to help!"

- A light bulb works well with the notion –

   "We need your bright ideas!"

It is important to involve the individuals who will be *benefiting* from the funds in the design of the recruiting materials. Use pictures drawn by students, or include a picture of some of the recipients of the funds. In the news business it is called "putting a face on the story." It is just as important that your recruiting efforts help to make a connection for your prospective volunteers.

One last note on materials: all of your recruiting materials need to include the organization's name, the purpose of the fund raiser, the type of help you need, the date of the function, and how to the contact someone to volunteer.

Got the What – Now for the WHO

The recruiting materials are done. Now who do you recruit? The best volunteers are the folks who feel they have a vested interest in the outcome of the event. People who have volunteered in the past are excellent resources. In organizations such as schools and churches, parents and extended family members of the students benefiting from the funds raised are a good place to start. Also, former students may be interested in giving a helping hand.

In other organizations current volunteers and people who have expressed an interest are a good group to begin with. Retirees make great volunteers but are often overlooked. There are plenty of these people who love to be involved with something but aren't always asked. The key point here is to broaden your thinking and don't leave out any possibilities.

Here are some other ideas:

- individual groups within churches are often looking for community outreach opportunities
- human resource managers in some organizations are interested in providing their employees with community outreach opportunities
- school and college alumni associations may have an interest in participating
- realtors will often support schools and churches in their areas
- contact your local chamber of commerce – they often look for volunteer opportunities for their members
- professional associations such as the Society for Human Resource Managers (SHRM) have committees that are tasked with identifying community outreach opportunities for their members

As you can see, there are many folks who want to get involved. Spend some time doing some brainstorming with your committee members to come up with a good list and start recruiting!

What and Who weren't so bad. How about HOW?

How do you go about recruiting? Talk to EVERYONE. We are connected to MANY more people than we think we are. Marketing pro's tell us that every person has a circle of some 250 people (on average) that we know and who know us well enough that we wouldn't mind calling them up on the phone. When you touch one of your 250 and they agree to touch theirs you've started multiplying the number of potential folks from which you can recruit. Experts say that we are only 6 layers of connection (6 degrees of separation) away from almost anyone on EARTH! Now, true… there will be overlap in who you know – particularly within the organization – but there will be strength in sharing the recruiting burden with those who will want help themselves and who know folks you don't know!

Start early and get your committee chairpersons in place. Once you do this, you will be able to enlist their help in securing volunteers for their specific committees. They will be very motivated to find help!!

Here are some successful approaches to use:

- Place an article in the organization's newsletter   - Plan early for this one. Identify the person who is responsible for submissions to the newsletter and get publication dates and requirements.

- Place an ad on the organization's website.

- Send flyers home with the beneficiaries – i.e. the scouts, choir members, school homework folders, etc.

- Make announcements at regularly scheduled meetings. Be sure to ask for a spot on the agenda.

- Got a directory? Great! Send out mailers – or better yet, place a call.

- Place notices, with permission of course, in the organization's high traffic areas.

- Secure a list of people involved in the organization and send an email request.

- Record some of the activities of the folks who will be recipients of the fund raiser and show this at a meeting or place it on the organization's website.

- Involve the recipients of the funds as much as you can. For example, students can be involved in a Spaghetti Dinner as the wait staff.

- Don't overlook the power of a party. Throw a little shindig – a pep-rally – for persons interested in supporting the cause. Punch and cookies, a meeting place, and a demo from the organization on what they are raising the money for is the total agenda. Sign-up sheets by committee can get the ball rolling. If yours is a BIG "Do" then you might even let the event committee chairperson's pitch their committee and the jobs they need done.

- Enlist the help of others. Tell **everyone** you know about the event and ask if they know of someone who might like to participate.

When recruiting in person, have a sign-up sheet handy so that folks can volunteer while it is fresh on their minds. Here is a sample:

(Name of the Event) Volunteer Sign-Up Sheet
Date of the Event

Committee Name	Volunteer's Name	Home Phone	Work Phone	Email Address
Publicity				
Live Auction				
Silent Auction				
Decorations				

NOTE:
> There are many people who would love to be asked, but don't always step up first. They might not even KNOW how much fun they could have. Make sure that people know that there is a job for everyone regardless of time or talents. In many cases, people have been attracted to an organization through a volunteer assignment and learn they have talents that they didn't know they had.

Screening and Selection

You may be thinking, "Why do I need to screen and select folks? If they reflect light – they are qualified!!!! I will be thrilled to death to have the help!"

While there is truth here, don't let your panic lead to decisions that will make more work for you later. For certain key positions, you need to be selective about who takes the assignment. The area of committee leadership is such a role. Remember, your goal as the event chairperson is to delegate as much as possible to your committees. So, you need to make certain that these folks have leadership skills and can run with things on their own.

In many instances you will know the individuals that you involve as committee chairpersons through other events in which you've been involved. You've seen them in action and know that they have the skills that you need for the role.

In the event that you haven't worked with someone in a volunteer capacity, here are a few questions you can ask when talking with them about the position you need filled.

1. *What types of volunteer work have you done in the past?*
   This question will give you an idea about the type of roles they may be interested in or for which they may be qualified.

2. *What did you enjoy the most about that volunteer assignment?*
   The answer to this question typically indicates their motivators.

3. *Is there anything you would do differently if you were to volunteer in that role again?*
   The response to this question can show one's ability to think through details and their desire to do a great job as a volunteer.

4. *What did you do that made you successful in that role?*
   Get ready to take notes! You'll probably hear some great ideas. Also, the response can tell you how they measure their success.

5. *How much time will you be able to commit to a volunteer assignment?*
   Willingness to commitment of time is extremely important when taking a leadership role. The volunteer needs to be clear on the amount of time that you think will be involved.

6. What is most important to you when working as a volunteer?
This information is good to have because you'll want to know how you an be a resource to this individual.

We aren't suggesting that you conduct a formal interview with people, but that you ask these types of questions in a conversational manner in person or over the phone. You also may want to create a questionnaire for them to complete and sell them on the idea of filling it out by letting them know that you want them to be in a role that they enjoy.

The key point here is to make certain that you have the **right** people in the **right** jobs. Success in this area will make a huge difference in the overall success of the event and your mental and physical well-being as Event Chairperson.

A Note about DIFFICULT PEOPLE:

We have a "Life's Too Short" list populated with folks we find hard to work with. One that comes to mind is a very powerful person with a lot of good ideas but she also feels a profound need to be indispensable. She will set up "failures" for others that she can rush in at the last minute and "rescue" everyone from. You probably have her clone somewhere in your organization. She's the one who thinks NOTHING should be spent on software, services, or help. She is even willing to accuse those who do of wasting the organization's resources... probably not to their faces though.

Beware of this person and her influence. Like "Marie Baronne" on **EVERYBODY LOVES RAYMOND**, she will act innocent and thoroughly offended if you catch her at her game. Mean people are good at accusing YOU of what they are doing – WHILE they do it! Better to recruit AROUND her or – at the very worst (for you) – give her a non-essential task that she will, doubtless, take a huge bow for. Sometimes these folks are gifted but just don't know how to work with others. If they can produce in a "going it solo" job like Treasurer or *maybe* Publicity then put her there and order extra bulbs for the spotlight.

No matter what strategy you use, life is too short to give your time and power to people who are willing and happy to abuse it. The "pearls before swine" admonition is true. They will trample your pearls... then attack you. Find nice people to play with.

Volunteer Orientation

Did you know that the number ONE REASON people don't do what you want them to do is that they DON'T KNOW WHAT YOU WANT or DON'T KNOW HOW to do it? It is true.

People work best when they know what is expected of them and have guidelines to follow. An orientation that provides the volunteers with the information that they need to be successful is very important.

An orientation for volunteers may take on several forms – a meeting, a letter, a checklist, an email, or a phone call. We recommend a meeting because the captured and focused energy of a group generates excitement and chatter about the event.

An orientation should consist of the following:

- The theme and date of the event – use the logo on everything!

- The financial goals of the event – generate excitement here!

- Expectations:
  o What they can expect from you, the Event Chairperson.
  o What you expect from them.
  o What they can expect to happen over the course of the timeline.

- Printed job descriptions.

- Time frames for completion of certain tasks (i.e. "Invitations must be mailed out no later than 4 weeks prior to the event.)

- The committee chairperson's contact information.

The orientation needs to be fun and motivating. Your objectives are to provide information and generate excitement about the event. Here are some ideas.

- Print an invitation to the meeting that goes along with the theme. For example, put the date and time of the meeting onto play money. This is very inexpensive and can be mailed or distributed in person easily. People love the look of money!

- Have upbeat music playing when people arrive. Often times, meetings will be held in the evening to accommodate volunteers who work outside the home during the day, so you want a quick "pick me up" when they enter the room.

- Wear something that goes along with the theme - such as a sailor's hat for a nautical theme.

- Decorate the room with the theme.

- Serve refreshments that go with the theme.

- Invite someone from the organization who will be benefiting from the funds to come and speak briefly about how the funds will be used.

- Give away a door prize. People love to win prizes! Hand each person a ticket or put a sticker on a printed agenda or a dot under a Chairperson (there are tons of ideas) to single out the winner. The door prize can be as simple as a giant candy bar that you can get at a dollar store.

- Hand out buttons or ribbons that indicate that they are volunteers and encourage them to wear them prior to the event for advertising. Wearing a button or ribbon will prompt people to ask questions about the event.

Volunteer Directory

Now that you have your volunteers, create a directory with your volunteers' contact information. The purpose of the directory is to give all volunteers on the event committees access to each other should they need assistance. Here's a sample format:

Parisian Nights Gala Volunteer Directory

Committee	Name	Address	Phone	Email
Decorations	Sue Smith, Chairperson	123 Main	218-444-0000	s@aol.com
	Vicky Jones	894 Smith	218-444-0000	v@aol.com
Silent Auction	Becky Lee Chairperson	555 Park	218-444-0000	b@aol.com
	Patti Jacks	520 Loop	218-444-0000	p@aol.com

You'll find that this directory is not only helpful for this year's event, but will be a great place to start recruiting for next year's event.

Volunteer Coordination and Accountability

Volunteers and leaders of volunteers have the right to certain expectations. Each person needs to feel ownership and to be held accountable for their role in the fund raising event.

The volunteer has the right to expect:*

- to be treated as a co-worker,
- to be given sufficient information, orientation and training for assignments,
- to be involved in a way that they are able to utilize their skills and talents,
- to have a written description of services to be performed, and,
- to be free to discuss problems, and make suggestions.

The volunteer director has the right to expect the volunteers:*

- to abide by his/her commitment,
- to discuss any problem encountered along the way,
- to cooperate with all committee members, and,
- to request clarification of an assignment.

* *Excerpted from the Volunteer Handbook of the State of Washington's Department of Social and Health Services.*

Motivating and Recognizing Volunteers

Every person who volunteers, regardless of the type of assignment, needs to feel appreciated. As you are going through the planning and execution phases of the event take time to let folks know that they are valued. There are so many ideas to choose from. Here are just a few.

- Acknowledge a list of volunteers as an article in the organization's newsletter. Make certain you have everyone's name!

- Send an email to all volunteers letting them know you appreciate their efforts and to keep up the great work.

- Small treats at meetings, such as a bag with a few homemade cookies, with bright curly ribbon.

- Have a wine and cheese party in your home halfway through your timeline just to say thanks and celebrate successes.

- Send an email card – they are free and very appreciated!

- Take pictures of the volunteers in action and post them so that they are noticed. If you use a digital camera, you can send them to each person in the photo electronically!

During the event, look for an appropriate time to have all of the volunteers to stand and receive applause. Thank your committee chairpersons after the event by hosting a small get-together or simply send them a thank-you note.

Host a gathering for all volunteers. It could simply be a meeting after the event to recap your success and give fun award certificates to the volunteers like this:

WE MADE OUR GOAL!!!

**Thanks to all our great supporters and our invaluable
volunteers for
St. John's BLACK AND WHITE BALL**

Your devotion is DEEPLY appreciated.

_____   _____
Chair Person   **Date**

We've given you a lot of ideas in this chapter. Find those that make
the most sense to you, implement them, or use some of the dozens that
popped into your mind as you read this chapter.

The most important points to take away from this chapter are to:

- spend time planning,

- get the word out to everyone,

- be selective about your committee chairpersons,

- make certain that all volunteers have the information they need
  to be successful, and

- ensure that each volunteer feels valued!!

Chapter 5

How many angels can dance on the head of a pin?

Event Committees

Have you ever been bitten by an elephant? How about a mosquito? For most people the answer to the first question is "No" and the second is "Yes." We all do a pretty good job of avoiding the huge threats in life. It's the little things we don't see coming that tend to get us. If you've lived long enough to volunteer to Chairperson a committee you know that it's the little details that can cause us the most problems. The good news is that the success is in the small details as well!!! Get all of them identified, done – and done WELL – and success is hard to avoid.

As the Event Chairperson, you will quickly find that having a group of enthusiastic, empowered, and informed volunteers, each focused on specific responsibilities, will make your life much easier, and will go a long way toward ensuring that your event is successful.

The activities associated with producing an event are typically the same regardless of the fundraiser, but the number of volunteers and committees needed to pull it off will differ depending on the size and scope of the event, and the number and experience of available volunteers.

As you prepare to recruit your committee chairpersons, look for these key qualities that will help them get their jobs done – and yours in the process:

- **Leadership skills** – the ability to motivate and get others involved in your cause

- **Organizational skills** – keeping accurate records, staying on task, and encourage others to do so

- **Commitment** – willingness to stay focused, set priorities, and get the job done

- **Enthusiasm** – exhibiting excitement about the organization and the fundraising event

- **Team Player** – pitching in where needed and not focused on his/her individual recognition

We've listed the specific committees here. Detailed chairperson job descriptions follow to help guide you in your planning.

Event Committees

Committee Name	Purpose
Program Advertising	solicit advertising dollars for the event program
Publicity	create an awareness of the event throughout the organization and the community
Underwriter Solicitation	solicit underwriting dollars for the event
Menu	plan the menu for the event
Decorations	assist in the development of the theme and create a themed- experience through the decorations for the event
Live Auction	solicit donations for the live auction and coordinate this component of the event
Silent Auction	solicit donations for the silent auction and coordinate this component of the event
Auction Check-in and Reception	greet event guests, collect payment for admission to the event, and provide guests with materials used during the event
Auction Check-out	collect payment and distribute auction items purchased as guests leave the event
Invitations/Reservations	• create and distribute invitations for the event • collect all reservations and monies of pre-paying guests and prepare guest list for the event
Program	create the program to include advertising, underwriter acknowledgement, description of auction items, and the agenda for the evening
Clean Up	ensure the clean up at the close of the event

Group Project Donations	generate interest in each beneficiary or group doing a project to donate for auction and coordinate the efforts of each
Thank-You	prepare and send thank-you notes to all donors
Treasurer	manage the financial aspects of the event

Event Chairperson

As the Event Chairperson, you are responsible for the success of the event. While this may seem overwhelming, you will be successful if you surround yourself with enthusiastic, qualified volunteers who share your vision. Once your committees are in place, your primary responsibilities include keeping the organizational leaders apprised of your progress throughout the planning process, providing guidance to your team and creating a motivating, enthusiastic experience for them. We've included some great ideas for volunteer motivation in Chapter 4.

As you move forward in your role, you may experience the feeling that it might be easier to do something yourself rather than passing the responsibility on to someone else. Avoid doing this at all costs! You'll not only become exhausted, you may miss out on wonderful ideas that others may have.

To illustrate this point, we asked several successful Event Chairpersons to give us some pearls of wisdom that we could pass on to you. Here are the highlights of their comments:

Be organized!
- Start early.
- Get a lot of folks to buy-in and support the event theme.
- Publicize like crazy!

Delegate!
- Surround yourself with people you can count on and…
- Let them go!

Always keep a smile on your face!
- Keep a positive attitude
- It's contagious!

Position title	Event Chairperson
Purpose of the position	Responsible for the planning and implementation of the fund-raising event
Activities/Job Description	<ul><li>create a theme for the event</li><li>work with organization to set the financial goal for the event</li><li>select the venue and menu</li><li>secure the entertainment</li><li>solicit volunteers</li><li>develop job descriptions for key volunteer roles</li><li>acts as liaison for organization – report on progress of event planning and execution.</li><li>provide direction to all committee chairpersons</li><li>hold committee meetings</li><li>set policy and provide guidance to all volunteers</li><li>set standards for the auction database</li><li>responsible for volunteer appreciation</li><li>works with treasurer to establish the budget</li><li>provide treasurer with receipts for all expenses incurred</li><li>create an Event Notebook detailing all activities and results</li></ul>
Approximate time commitment	10 -15 hours a week prior to the event. 4 - 5 hours the day of the event

Program Advertising Chairperson

The Program Advertising Chairperson is primarily responsible for raising money to cover costs for the event through the sale of ads for the event program.

Through this type of solicitation, individuals and businesses are given the opportunity to make a charitable donation by purchasing an ad in the event program.

There are two types of advertising – personal (no, not that kind!), and commercial. Personal ads may congratulate an individual or a group for specific accomplishments. Some businesses may not have a product that lends itself to being donated, so purchasing advertising is a good alternative.

Specific ideas for soliciting for advertising dollars are found in Chapters 10 & 12.

Position title	**Program Advertising Chairperson**
Purpose of the position	Responsible for securing advertising and underwriting dollars for the event.
Activities/Job Description	<ul><li>set goal for advertising dollars</li><li>set the size, layouts, and price for ads in conjunction with the program chairperson</li><li>sell advertising for the event program</li><li>collect ad copy and money from advertisers</li><li>provide the program chairperson with all graphics for ads, copy, etc. by printing deadline</li><li>send tear sheets (copies of the printed ad) or a program to advertisers</li><li>provide treasurer with receipts for all expenses incurred</li><li>write notes for the Event Notebook and give them to Event Chairperson</li></ul>
Approximate time commitment	4 - 5 hours a week prior to the printing of the program.

Underwriter Solicitation Chairperson

The Underwriter Solicitation Chairperson is primarily responsible for raising money to cover costs for the event.

Through this type of solicitation, individuals and businesses are given the opportunity to make a charitable donation by underwriting designated costs of the event.

Because this individual will be contacting high ranking officials within organizations, it is important that he/she be well schooled in business etiquette and have a professional demeanor.

Specific ideas for soliciting for underwriting dollars are found in Chapters 10 and 12.

Position title	Underwriter Solicitation Chairperson
Purpose of the position	Responsible for securing underwriting dollars for the event.
Activities/Job Description	<ul><li>set goal for underwriting dollars</li><li>solicit underwriting dollars from local businesses and members of the organization</li><li>provide the Program Chairperson with all underwriters' information by printing deadline</li><li>send a program to underwriters</li><li>organize a pre-event party, reception, or cocktail hour for underwriters</li><li>purchase gifts for underwriters</li><li>coordinate choice table assignments for underwriters with the reservations chairperson</li><li>provide treasurer with receipts for all expenses incurred</li><li>write notes for the Event Notebook and give them to Event Chairperson</li></ul>
Approximate time commitment	4 - 5 hours a week prior to the printing of the program.

Publicity Chairperson

"Getting the word out" and creating a "buzz" is the responsibility of the Publicity Chairperson. To be successful, publicity should be approached with a plan that includes a variety of media. More on this in Chapter 9.

One of the advantages you have in this role is that you can be supported through the efforts of everyone in the organization. As a result, your primary activities are to create the publicity plan, arrange for printing and distribute throughout the organization for placement in pre-designated media and physical locations.

After the event, your final publicity will be announcing the results.

Position title	**Publicity Chairperson**
Purpose of the position	Responsible for all publicity leading up to and following the event
Activities/Job Description	<ul><li>create publicity for students, faculty, families, and the community</li><li>arrange for publicity to be printed and distributed</li><li>update list of items for the live and silent auctions and publicize</li><li>publicize the event again after the invitation mailing (as event nears) to encourage potential attendees to purchase their tickets</li><li>make certain that all publicity is theme-related</li><li>create and disseminate final publicity about the results of the event</li><li>provide treasurer with receipts for all expenses incurred</li><li>write notes for the Event Notebook and give them to Event Chairperson</li></ul>
Approximate time commitment	2 - 3 hours a week prior to the event and 1 – 2 hours following the event.

Decorations Chairperson

The Decorations Chairperson sets the tone and ambiance of the event. In some cases you may find that decorations are not considered to be important. However, without them the event is like eating cake with no frosting. It tastes okay, but it's not memorable. As a result, you may find that you'll need to sell others on the importance of exceeding expectations of your guests by setting, "just the right mood."

As you begin your planning you'll work with the Event Chairperson to set the theme. There are so many wonderful themes from which to choose. You'll want to consider the decorations prior to making your final decision on the theme. Another point to consider is the amount of money you are trying to raise. The budget for decorations should be directly proportionate to the amount of the funds you want to raise. Chapter 7 will give you some direction here.

Your goal as you plan is to create an environment that results in guests saying, "Wow" from the moment they check in and throughout the evening. Look for theme and decoration ideas in Chapter 8.

Position Title	Decorations Chairperson
Purpose of the position	Responsible for all decorations relating to the event
Activities/Job Description	<ul><li>work with event chairperson on theme</li><li>work with treasurer and event chairperson to determine the budget</li><li>design decorations for the dining tables, the entrance, the auction locations, check-in table</li><li>gather all materials for the decorations</li><li>provide decorations for any activities prior to the event as needed</li><li>determine price of decorations if they are to be sold or raffled after the event</li><li>decorate the day of the event</li><li>collect any remaining decorations at the end of the event</li><li>provide treasurer with receipts for all expenses incurred</li><li>write notes for the Event Notebook and give to the Event Chairperson</li></ul>
Approximate time commitment	2 - 3 hours a week prior to the event and 4 – 5 hours the day of the event. This will vary based upon the complexity of the decorations.

Live Auction Chairperson

The Live Auction Chairperson is responsible for acquiring high value items that your audience will find reasonable to bid higher sums on.

As you begin your planning consider the audience and brainstorm with others on the types of items you want to go after. When you secure items that match the attendees' interest, the bidding will be lively and will result in high dollars.

Your other responsibilities primarily involve the logistics associated with preparing and conducting the Live Auction.

Position Title	Live Auction Chairperson
Purpose of the position	Responsible for all securing donated items and set-up for the Live Auction
Activities/Job Description	<ul><li>set goal for number of items for the live auction</li><li>solicit donations</li><li>assemble donation forms in Donations Notebook and set minimum bids</li><li>book the auctioneer</li><li>create a database of donations, donors and contact information</li><li>assign an auction identification number to each donation</li><li>collect donation forms and set minimum bids</li><li>determine the order of the auction items</li><li>secure props for the auction items</li><li>secure auction paddles for the live auction and give to the auction check-in and reception chairperson</li><li>prepare the written description of auction items</li><li>provide the publicity chairperson with the list of auction items for ads to publicity</li><li>provide the auctioneer with a script that describes each item in the order they are to be auctioned</li><li>prepare live auction bid sheets in triplicate</li><li>provide treasurer with receipts for all expenses incurred</li><li>write notes for the Event Notebook and give to the Event Chairperson</li></ul>
Approximate time commitment	8 – 10 hours a week prior to the event 2 - 3 hours the day of the event.

Silent Auction Chairperson

The Silent Auction Chairperson is responsible for acquiring donated items that will purchased by guests. In addition, you will be helping the Live Auction Chairperson determine items that would bring more money through live bidding.

One way to get started on your donations is to make a list of items that you want to go after. As a rule of thumb, use yourself as a guide to help you decide which items that people will want to bid on.

Another key responsibly is to create a Silent Auction area that is appealing and user friendly. You want the arrangement of the items to draw people in and the actual bidding process to be easy.

Position Title	Silent Auction Chairperson
Purpose of the position	Responsible for securing donations and set-up for the Silent Auction
Activities/Job Description	<ul><li>solicit for silent auction donations</li><li>assemble donation forms in Donations Notebook</li><li>arrange for donations to be picked up and stored prior to the event</li><li>create a database of donations, donors and contact information</li><li>assign an auction identification number to each donation</li><li>create a description bid sheet along with a minimum bid for each item</li><li>print the bid sheet in triplicate (one copy to stays with item, one goes to winning bidder and one for records)</li><li>prepare envelopes for each donation that involve gift certificates and give them to the auction check-out chairperson on the day of the event</li><li>arrange to have props (eye catching stage dressing) for all items</li><li>periodically provide the publicity chairperson with an updated list of auction items</li><li>secure transportation of items to and from venue</li><li>work with event chairperson for the design of the silent auction area</li><li>set up silent auction on the day of the event</li><li>follow-up with people who left the event early without paying for their purchase to collect their money</li><li>provide treasurer with receipts for incurred expenses</li><li>write notes for the Event Notebook and give to Event Chairperson</li></ul>
Approximate time commitment	8 – 10 hours a week prior to the event. 4 - 5 hours the day of the event.

Auction Check-In and Reception Chairperson

The main function of this job is to make certain that all guests, whether pre-registered or not, have the materials they need during the evening.

In addition, you and your committee members will be the first impression guests will have of the evening ahead. So surround yourself with friendly, outgoing people.

Position Title	Auction Check-In and Reception Chairperson
Purpose of the position	Responsible for greeting and checking-in guests at the event
Activities/Job Description	<ul><li>work with Invitations/Reservation Chairperson to compile a list of people who have purchased advanced tickets to the event</li><li>prepare name tags for guests</li><li>work with the Treasurer to determine what you will need in order to collect cash, checks, and credit card payments</li><li>give the Treasurer all collected monies and credit card payments</li><li>create a process for walk in guests</li><li>prepare check-in packets for guests to include things like a program, raffle tickets, a live auction paddle, bidder number or bar code stickers if using AuctionStar®, etc.</li><li>arrange for volunteers to greet and check-in guests</li><li>set up check–in table near the entrance of the venue on the day of the event</li><li>welcome each guest</li><li>provide Treasurer all receipts for incurred expenses</li><li>write notes for the Event Notebook and give to the Event Chairperson</li></ul>
Approximate time commitment	8 – 10 hours prior to the event and 1 – 2 hours the day of the event.

Auction Check-Out Chairperson

This job is not to be taken lightly. Just as the check-in experience is the first impression guests have of the event, the check-out experience is the last impression they leave with. So your job is to make sure that your guests leave with the desire to attend the event again next year. More suggestions of how to accomplish this can be found in Chapter 14.

Position Title	**Auction Check-Out Chairperson**
Purpose of the position	Responsible for collecting payments for all auction items purchased
Activities/Job Description	• secure a list of all live and silent auction items from the appropriate chairpersons • work with the Treasurer to determine what you will need in order to collect cash, checks, and credit card payments • set up check–out tables near the exit of the venue on the day of the event • provide each purchaser with cash receipts if applicable • thank each purchaser for their support • enter dollar amounts for each item sold on the list of donated items • provide all receipts for any incurred expenses to the Treasurer • give the Treasurer all collected monies and credit card payments • prepare a report of all monies received, list any outstanding payments to be made and give to Silent Auction Chairperson • write notes for the Event Notebook and give to the Event Chairperson
Approximate time commitment	2 – 3 hours prior to the event, 1 – 2 hours on the day of the event and 2 – 3 hours after the event.

Invitations/Reservations Chairperson

The Invitations/Reservations Chairperson is responsible for inviting guests to the event. Invitations are the first impression of the event and in some instances the organization. Though this job may seem to be insignificant, it is every bit as important as a receptionist in a major corporation. When the guest receives the invitation, you want them to recognize that the organization is professional and legitimate. Your goal with the invitation is to create an interest and excitement about the event.

The Reservations part of the role is important in the final countdown for the event. As guests respond to the invitation, your key responsibilities are to make certain that each guest has submitted payment and that you have the correct spelling of each attendee's name. Finally, you will be responsible for the table assignment for guests.

As the chairperson for this committee, plan to participate in creating the theme so that the invitation represents it well.

Position Title	Invitations/Reservations Chairperson
Purpose of the position	Responsible for the design and distribution of the invitations to the event
Activities/Job Description	<ul><li>work with the Event and Decorations Chairpersons to establish a theme</li><li>create a mailing list of prospective attendees</li><li>design the invitations</li><li>print the invitations</li><li>create a reservations card, if applicable</li><li>mail/distribute the invitations according to the event's timeline</li><li>collect guest reservations</li><li>send acknowledgement of receipt of reservation as necessary</li><li>create a list of pre-paid guests along with any specified seating assignments, if applicable and give to Check-in Chairperson</li><li>give the Treasurer all collected monies prior to the event</li><li>provide the Treasurer receipts for printed materials and postage</li><li>write notes for the Event Notebook and give to the Event Chairperson</li></ul>
Approximate time commitment	15-20 hours prior to the event for Invitations. 5-6 hours prior to the event for Reservations.

Program Chairperson

As the Program Chairperson, your main responsibility is to create an event program that is attractive, easy to read, organized, accurate, and cost effective for the event.

In addition, you will be responsible for making certain that all advertisers receive copies of their ads and all donors are given recognition in the program.

Chapter 12 discusses the development of the program.

Position Title	Program Chairperson
Purpose of the position	Responsible for the design and printing of the event programs
Activities/Job Description	<ul><li>work with the Event Chairperson / Decorations and Invitations/Reservations Chairperson to design the cover of the program</li><li>select and work with the printer on the overall design requirements (if applicable)</li><li>gather descriptions of donated auction items from the Live and Silent Auction Chairpersons</li><li>type the program</li><li>coordinate advertising space and underwriter acknowledgement with the Ads & Underwriter Chairperson</li><li>coordinate printing of programs according to event timeline</li><li>provide tear sheets (copies of the ads) to the Ads and Underwriter Chairperson</li><li>give printed programs to the Auction Check-In and Reception Chairperson prior to the night of the event</li><li>provide the Treasurer receipts for incurred expenses</li><li>write notes for the Event Notebook and give to the Event Chairperson</li></ul>
Approximate time commitment	20-30 hours prior to the event.

Clean-Up Chairperson

The Clean-up Chairperson oversees the clean-up activities after the event is over. Typically, your key responsibilities are to make certain that all event-related items are taken out of the venue. In most instances, if your event is being held in rented space such as a country club or hotel, cleaning the room is part of the package.

If you are hosting the event in a private facility such as a church or school, you may need to pull a group of folks together to actually clean up everything and put chairs and tables away. Most people are willing, but typically do not volunteer for this committee, so get your recruiting hat on!

Position Title	Clean-Up Chairperson
Purpose of the position	Responsible for the clean-up activities associated with the event
Activities/Job Description	<ul><li>solicit volunteers for help with clean-up</li><li>work with Event Chairperson to determine what clean up responsibilities are expected by the venue</li><li>coordinate clean-up activities after the event</li><li>provide Treasurer receipts for incurred expenses</li><li>write notes for the Event Notebook and give to the Event Chairperson</li></ul>
Approximate time commitment	2 – 3 hours prior to the event and 1 – 2 hours after the event

Group Project/Donations Chairperson

This position is typically utilized when raising money for a school or church. Classes or groups will either put a project together, such as making a quilt, or they will pool their money and donate something.

Your responsibility is to coordinate these projects and donations by working with teachers or individuals leading the groups. Because there are many activities going on, you'll find that you will need to do some gentle prodding to make certain that deadlines are met.

Position Title	Group Project/Donations Chairperson
Purpose of the position	Responsible for coordinating the donations from each group that will benefit from the fundraiser
Activities/Job Description	<ul><li>work with Event Chairperson to identify the classes or groups that will be providing a donation.</li><li>identify a contact person for each group project donation</li><li>work with the contact person to coordinate the completion of the donation against the event timeline</li><li>arrange to take pictures of the groups and include them with the donated project (if desired)</li><li>provide the Silent Auction and/or Live Auction Chairpersons with the descriptions of the donations</li><li>ensure there are donor forms for every group item and file one copy in Silent and/or Live Auction Donation's Notebooks</li><li>arrange for the donations to be transported to the venue or put in storage prior to the event</li><li>provide Treasurer receipts for incurred expenses</li><li>write notes for the Event Notebook and give to the Event Chairperson</li></ul>
Approximate time commitment	10 – 12 hours prior to the event and 1 – 2 hours the day of the event

Thank-You Chairperson

As the Thank-You Chairperson, your role is to ensure that all donors, advertisers, and underwriters receive thank-you letters. In most cases, these letters are done at the end of the event; however, you may find it easier to do them as you receive the donations. You'll work closely with the Live Auction, Silent Auction, and Ads and Underwriter Chairpersons to collect all of the donors' names and addresses.

Position Title	Thank-You Chairperson
Purpose of the position	Responsible for sending thank-you notes to all donors for the event.
Activities/Job Description	<ul><li>work with Event Chairperson to create a thank-you letter that can be used for all donors</li><li>secure the donations database from the Live and Silent Auction Chairpersons and the Ads and Underwriter Chairperson</li><li>prepare and mail thank-you letters for each donor, advertiser, and underwriter</li><li>provide Treasurer receipts for incurred expenses</li><li>write notes for the Event Notebook and give to the Event Chairperson</li></ul>
Approximate time commitment	The time frame for this role is directly proportionate to the number of donations. To avoid an overwhelming task, send thank- you notes periodically as you receive donations.

Treasurer

Your role as Treasurer is an important one. Initially, you will work with the Event Chairperson to finalize the budget and establish the policy and procedures for expense reimbursements. During the course of the planning, your key responsibility will be to collect receipts, and to track and reimburse expenses. Upon the completion of the event, you will collect all monies, deposit them and prepare a financial report that indicates total dollars collected, final expenses, and the net profit for the event.

Position Title	Treasurer
Purpose of the position	Responsible for all financial aspects of the event
Activities/Job Description	• arrange for a checking account and set up check signing privileges • work with Event Chairperson to establish a budget for the event • prepare the budget and distribute to committee chairpersons • Establish and distribute a reimbursement policy for volunteers and distribute • collect and pay all invoices for the event • collect all receipts for incurred expenses and reimburse volunteers • provide Auction Check-In and Auction Check-Out Chairpersons with cash box and a credit card validator, if applicable • collect and deposit all monies from auction and ticket sales • prepare a profit and loss statement and give to the Event Chairperson • write notes for the Event Notebook and give to the Event Chairperson
Approximate time commitment	10 – 12 hours prior to the event and 10 to 12 hours after the event.

Now, you've got your list of committees and the chairpersons' job descriptions. It's time to recruit! Select great folks to help you and you will find your job as Event Chairperson extremely rewarding and fun – and much easier!

Even with this thorough list of committee chairperson responsibilities, you may find that your individual event calls for an additional committee – or the size and scope of the event make you think you should split one of the duties into two. We've placed a job description form on the website to help you detail those jobs. You remember…

www.storymasterpress.com/auctionhelp

Chapter 6

How do I get all these people to do all of these jobs?

Committee Meetings

As the planning for your event unfolds, you'll spend many hours in meetings. Our guess is that you will have other things going on besides this event so it makes sense to make the most of every meeting. The purpose of this chapter is to provide you with some suggestions on holding successful – and shorter – meetings.

To make certain that all of your meetings are well attended, and accomplish your objectives, follow these steps:

Step One – Set a place and time that is as convenient as possible for most participants. Make it as a *routine meeting time*. This approach will ensure better attendance.

> Note: There may be some volunteers who can't attend any meetings, but still are able to help. Keep them in the loop by sending them copies of the minutes of each meeting through email.

Step Two – Announce the meeting through a variety of methods:
- put a notice in the organization's newspaper
- hand out a list of meeting dates and times at your initial meeting
- use email reminders

Step Three –Set expectations and outcomes for each meeting. Let attendees know what the objectives are for the meeting and what you hope to accomplish as a result of the meeting. When the attendees expectations are set, they will come to the meeting more prepared.

Step Four – And without question the most important thing you can do to make the meeting effective is to - PREPARE AN AGENDA! Think we're over-stressing a piece of paper? It probably sounds like a major yawn, but a written agenda has enormous power over the flow of a meeting. When Shirley "I have an idea" tries to pull you off task with her pet project you can say, "That sounds like something we need to discuss in detail. Let's put that under New Business." Then when it comes time for New Business you can discuss it or decide to hand it to a committee to yammer on about until everyone feels like they've had a lobotomy.

We consider the agenda to be the best way to make sure that you stay on task during your meeting and the strongest tool for minimizing distractions and 'chasing rabbits.' Put an agenda together with topics to discuss and the *allotted time to discuss them*. Remember, YOU are in control. If, in the meeting, you decide you need more time – take it. If not… you have it in writing – "We don't have time for that now… Let's let the (fill in the blank) committee iron that out and report to us at our next meeting." Then, distribute the agenda to your committee chairpersons prior to the meeting to make certain that all discussion items are noted. You may also want to distribute a copy of the agenda during the meeting if you feel it will help keep things on task.

Here is a sample of an agenda that you can follow as a guide:

Meeting Agenda

1. Opening Comments
   - objectives of the meeting
   - discuss the agenda

2. Committee Updates
   - accomplishments to date
   - current activities
   - need help with…

3. New Business

4. Questions/Answers

5. Develop Next Meeting Agenda Items

6. Meeting Adjourned

To download a free digital copy of this format, go to
www.storymasterpress.com/auctionhelp.

As the chairperson for the event, you'll be hosting the initial pre-planning meeting with all interested parties. Your objectives for this meeting are:

- Discuss & finalize venue options.
- Discuss volunteer opportunities where people are needed. Provide a synopsis of each committee's responsibilities. An example of a synopsis is provided in Chapter 5.
- If spots are open for committee chairpersons, ask for volunteers and finalize at the meeting (You may have people in mind for these positions based upon previous experiences together. As a result, most spots will be filled prior to this meeting. In the event that they are, introduce the chairpersons to the group.)
- Announce the theme for the event.
- Discuss soliciting donations and ask the group for personal donations.

After this initial meeting, you will set specific objectives based upon what you need to accomplish. The timeline in Chapter 1 will help you to develop agenda items and schedule future meetings.

Appoint a Corresponding Secretary to take and distribute the minutes of your meetings. This person is critical to your ability to keep committee members who may have missed a meeting informed. To make this job easier, suggest the minutes be typed and distribute them through email.

Chapter 7

What do we spend money for, and when do we beg?

The Event Budget

The event budget is a map for all the expenses that will occur during the process of planning and putting on the event. With good planning every dollar spent can be accounted for before the money is spent. It is so much easier to manage the event's expenses when you document all the potential costs at the outset of planning. For example... Ask yourself, "How much do I want to spend on the invitations? Are we going to spend $2.00 each, including the stamp, or are we thinking about running a master copy and distributing them through the members of the organization which will cost pennies."

Giving direction to the committee chairpersons is vital to maintaining and watching your spending. Often times the chairperson of a committee will have a history of working in an assigned area and can help with budget amounts. Realistic expectations of the cost of putting on a function have to be considered. Asking the chairperson how much they think they will need is one way to come up with a budget. You have the authority to overrule their spending requests, if you don't agree. Be sure to give ownership of managing each area's budget to the volunteers and chairpersons. Ownership helps people understand they have a vested interest, which can lead to good decision-making and will help them understand the overall vision of the event.

Documentation of the budget is very important to prepare for successful events to come. The future planners can draw upon your good and thorough record keeping. They can then plan for expenses they might not otherwise have been able to foresee.

Creating the Budget

Determine a total amount that is reasonable for the overall earning potential of the event. Once a goal has been set you can then back into the budget. The event history with detailed spending records is the best information for you to use. If a budget history is not available then some research by the event or budget chairperson will be necessary. What do invitations cost? Are we printing them or are we making copies? If this is the first time the event has been tackled, then be very conservative with the budget.

The potential earnings will dictate some of the decisions as to how money will be spent. If your earnings potential is over $5000, the look and feel of a professional invitation states that the event is well-planned and that the monetary goals for the fundraiser are substantial.

To make this daunting task seem easier, and more accurate, ask committee chairpersons to submit their budgets to you as early as possible. Suggest that they do some brainstorming with their committee members to come up with realistic numbers.

Consider each of these categories below as you begin your planning.

- printing costs
- invitations - to include reservation cards if used
- programs
- publicity posters
- event signage
- flyers
- donor forms (in triplicate)
- bid sheets (in duplicate if bids are hand-written)
- description of items sheets/stationery
- table reservation cards
- thank-you note cards or stationery
- name tags
- organization's stationery & envelopes
- printer ink – black and color
- specialty paper for Live & Silent Auctions

Decorations
- materials for decorations
- balloons and helium (if desired)

Postage
- invitations & reservation cards
- thank-you letters
- solicitation letters
- all correspondence

Live Auction
- professional booking fee for auctioneer
- dry erase board and markers for the Big Board
- auction paddles

Silent Auction
- pencils & pens
- props
- stands for item descriptions
- 9 x 12 envelopes
- specialty papers for printing
- receipt books

Group Project
- materials needed to build the project (if the project is not underwritten)

Venue and Menu
- room rental
- food and beverages
- gratuity
- bartender
- audio/visual equipment (projectors, microphones, speakers, etc.)
- valet parking (optional)

Entertainment
- musicians
- DJ

- dance floor set-up fee

Auction Database
- software initial cost and licensing fees (if applicable)
- computer equipment rental (if applicable)

Underwriters
- gifts
- pre-event reception

There are other types of expenses that will be incurred based upon your event. It's a good idea to budget a little over what you think you'll need in each category to cover any extra expenses that may occur.

The bottom line is, the purpose of the event is to make as much money as possible. So, spend what is necessary to make the event memorable and profitable. The best budget is one paid for by advertising and underwriting. So, prepare your budget prior to soliciting your advertisers and underwriters and establish a minimum of 10% over your estimated budget costs as your goal for these dollars. A budget worksheet can be downloaded for free... guess where! Go to www.storymasterpress.com/auctionhelp.

The Profit and Loss Statement
Once the event is over you'll need to report your final earnings to your organization. This is typically called an Earnings Report or a Profit and Loss Statement (P&L). For our purposes, we'll refer to it as the P&L. This report lists the funds that were generated by ticket sales, auction sales, ads, donations and underwriting dollars and subtracts the total expenses to arrive at the total funds raised and is prepared by the Treasurer. This report is important to evaluate this event's results and to plan for the next year.

Here is a sample:

Parisian Nights Gala
P & L Statement
January, 2004

Income

Ticket Sales	$5,000.00
Silent Auction Sales	$10,000.00
Live Auction Sales	$20,000.00
Underwriting Dollars	$8,000.00
Advertising Sales	$2,500.00
Donations	$800.00
Total Income	$46,300.00

Expenses

Printing Costs	$1,000.00
Decorations	$500.00
Postage	$250.00
Live Auction Expenses	$800.00
Silent Auction Expenses	$250.00
Venue and Menu	$4,000.00
Entertainment	$350.00
Total Expenses	$7,150.00
Total Income	$39,150.00

If you are using auction software, this report will be generated automatically.

Chapter 8

Somehow Pompeii Nights just doesn't do it for me.

The Event Theme and Decorations

Setting the theme for your event is a critical step in the planning process. Once set, the theme is the foundation upon which your event is built. EVERY decision can be guided or influenced by the theme.

There are several things to consider regarding your theme. First, connect the purpose of the event, when possible, to the theme. For example, if you are raising money for students to go on a trip, consider a travel theme or the locations(s) to which they will be traveling. The obvious joke notwithstanding, "Pompeii Nights" might be JUST the way to put a positive and light spin when raising funds to rebuild after a disaster.

Second, consider involving the recipients of the funds in developing the theme. If raising funds for a school, involve the students. One idea that works well is to create a contest and award a prize for the best idea. For example, we have awarded a $25 gift certificate to a local mall and the student was recognized during the school announcements.   In addition to the theme, we have also involved the students in designing the logo.   If you use this approach, be sure to give some good guidelines to follow.

A third approach is to involve your committee chairpersons in a brainstorming session. Give everyone a "heads up" that you'll be using this approach at an initial meeting and ask the attendees to bring a few ideas with them. An important point about brainstorming – treat **every** idea as a good one and build on each idea presented. This simple tip will encourage the flow of ideas and you will end up with many from which to choose.

The number of themes is endless and we could fill this book up with them. Here are just a few that have worked very well for all different types of events.

- Western
- Nautical/Cruise
- Travel
- Circus
- City Lights
- Fishing for our Future
- Safari
- Casino Party
- Sock Hop
- Hollywood Nights
- Fall Harvest
- Beach
- Tropical Luau

As we pointed out, the event theme has an affect on the decorations, invitations, menu and venue, so choose it carefully. Whether your theme is formal or casual, spend as much time as necessary to select the right one and have fun!

Decorations

The decorations for your event can be as elaborate or simple as your budget allows. Decorations create the ambience for the event and should support the theme. At a minimum, you should decorate the following areas:

- entrance into your function
- centers of tables
- silent auction area
- dance area (if applicable)
- dining Area

In addition to the above, you may choose to add some of these ideas:

- name card placeholders
- party favors/mementos
- cityscapes or wall murals
- standup figures such as life-sized cardboard movie stars

One of the best ways to defray the costs of the decorations is to sell the table centerpieces. With this objective, you'll want to design your centerpieces so that people will have an interest in purchasing them. Discreetly place a price and item number on the centerpiece once it is on the table. People interested in purchasing the centerpieces can sign up for them on the appropriate bid sheet in the Silent Auction area.

Using balloons is another way to maximize your decorations dollars. Balloons are fairly inexpensive and add a lot of volume.

If you budget is limited, table centerpieces can be raffled to the guest to help defray the costs or underwritten as a simple way for a small business to participate at a controlled cost. Also consider using balloons. They add a lot of volume and are very inexpensive.

Here are some theme ideas with suggestions for invitations and decorations:

Western Theme

Invitation Idea: White paper with bandana or denim ribbon.

Decorations: OK Corral entrance for guests with a desert mural on the wall. Add some straw bales and some cactus. Table decorations could include mini-cowboy hats for name cards, a straw bale centerpiece with balloons attached and bandanas for napkins.

Tropical Theme

Invitation Idea: Bright neon colored paper with raffia.

Decorations: Have your guest enter through a Tiki Hut. Use lots of raffia, some palm trees, leis, Tiki torches, and Tiki masks and you've got yourself an island get-away! Table decorations could include Tiki molded candles, hibiscus floating candles, pineapple and fresh fruit. Lots of bright colors like lime green, yellow and orange are just perfect!

Celestial Theme

Invitation Idea: A clear envelope with star studded confetti holds the invitation.

Decorations: This theme can be used with moonlight and stars, the galaxy, Hollywood stars and Stargate. Dress the entrance with a giant star through which your guests can enter. Dress the table with 3D stars in gold, silver and black surrounded by shiny confetti. Put lots of silver, gold, and black pearlized balloons around the room.

Under Construction

This theme works very well when you are raising money to build something. Be sure to ask your contractor to donate items for the decorations.

Invitation Idea: Construction signs

Decorations: Make table centerpieces with flashing warning lights along with standing construction signage ie. Danger, Hard Hat Area, Toxic Waste, Warning, Wet Paint. Use paint buckets for floral arrangements and paint stir sticks can be used for auction paddles. Construction stickers are available for the nametags. For fun, ask attendees to dress the part.

Getting Down To Business

Chapter 9

How are people going to know about this shindig?

Publicity

Publicity is defined as attracting public interest. The success of your event is based upon the number of guests you have and their willingness to bid. There are lot of factors that play into this, such as the attraction of the auction items, but you have to get people to your event first. Publicity is also done after the event is over. This type of publicity gives information regarding the success of the event.

There are three key objectives in planning for your publicity. You want to

- create an awareness about your organization's fund raising needs,
- communicate information regarding your event, and
- generate excitement and enthusiasm about attending the event.

Typically, publicity for these types of events is done through traditional advertising, organization-wide communication and word-of-mouth. Let's take a look at each one.

Traditional Advertising

Traditional advertising is done outside of the organization. Print and radio advertising are a couple of avenues to consider.

Print Advertising

Print advertising consists of newspaper articles and posters. An effective approach to advertising in the newspaper is through an article about your organization noting the particulars of your event. This generates a "heads up" to people who may have an interest in your organization and also contributes to the name recognition of the event. Articles appearing in small neighborhood newspapers are very effective. Look in neighborhood newspapers that are in your target area to identify the contact person for the placement of articles. Contact the appropriate person and ask for a copy of their editorial calendar. This calendar will give you the dates that you need to submit your pre-event and post-event articles.

In some instances, the newspaper may want to interview someone and take pictures. To be prepared for this opportunity, appoint a spokesperson for the event and gather his or her contact information. If the article includes a picture, give some thought to the type of picture that exemplifies your organization and is eye catching. Prior to agreeing to this type of publicity, check with your organization to get information regarding their protocol in this area and get proper clearance.

Event posters are a simple way to advertise. Posters can be printed and distributed to the members of the organization for distribution. The look of the poster is extremely important. In many instances, this poster may be the first impression of the event.

As you begin planning the layout of your posters, consider all the of ways that you can communicate the theme of the event. You may want to involve the organization's members in designing the artwork. Particularly if the organization has children, it's a great idea to get them to submit art and select the best. If you use this approach, be sure to include the artist's signature and age. This gives the event a personal touch while still looking professional.

Posters are placed both inside and outside of the organization's facility. Prior to printing, list the locations where you want to place the posters. This exercise will help you determine the amount and the size of the posters needed. The cost of professionally printed posters typically could be a determining factor in your distribution. Printing is a numbers game. As the numbers of posters printed increases, the cost per poster decreases. Don't scrimp in this area. In addition to giving the particulars of your event, the poster will also create name recognition each time it is seen. As in all of your expenses, try to get the printing donated and ensure that the printer gets plenty of publicity.

Radio Advertising

Radio advertising is primarily good for name recognition. The cost of radio advertising is very expensive, so contact stations that you believe reach the folks that you want and ask for donated air time. Many stations will give public announcements if plenty of notice is given. If you are unsuccessful in getting air time donated, you may want to focus your energy on other means of publicity.

Organization-wide Communication

Organization-wide communication is your best avenue for publicity. It is here that people have a vested interest in your event. In addition to letting folks know about the event, this type of publicity is best suited for generating enthusiasm about the auction items donated.

Publicity in the organization generally consists of flyers, the organization's newsletter, verbal announcements, the organization's website, invitations and email.

Flyers

Flyers are inexpensive and can be mass produced. Typically, they are copied vs. professionally printed and done on brightly colored paper to attract attention. Even though the cost is nominal, the message and the way the flyers look should be as carefully thought out as your professionally printed posters. Check for accuracy in every detail and avoid distributing flyers that are copied poorly. Because they are so inexpensive, they can be distributed as often as weekly. Later in this chapter, we offer some ideas on the distribution of flyers.

The Organization's Newsletter

Most organizations have a newsletter. Contact the publisher of the newsletter to determine publication dates, article length and cut-off dates for submission. There is usually no charge for this type of publicity, so use it as often as you can. If you have the opportunity to include several articles prior to the event, create a teaser at the end of each to get the readers to look for the articles in following newsletters. Here is an example of this type of teaser: *"Be sure to look for our top 10 auction items in the next edition of this newsletter!"*

Verbal Announcements

Verbal announcements can be made in person, over a loud speaker and via voice mail. The announcement should be interesting and should be delivered with enthusiasm. The announcement should be **well written** and **rehearsed** to avoid the perception that the announcer is "winging it".

If the announcement is being made in person, do something creative to generate interest in the message. For example, a boa and sunglasses are great costume pieces to wear to announce the event themed "The Bright Lights of Broadway".

If the announcement is being made over a loud speaker, consider doing it in verse or use an accent that supports the theme. How about singing the information to a recognizable tune?

In many schools, messages are recorded by the principal and then sent to each parent's home phone to get information out about a variety of subjects. In our experience, this is typically done in the evening or on the weekend in an effort to reach parents at home. If you choose to use this approach, limit the message. You may simply want to let them know that the event is coming and to look for the announcement in an upcoming newsletter. Check with your principal's office to see if this opportunity exists.

Regardless of your method, the announcement should be delivered succinctly and in such a way that it creates a desire in the listener to hear more.

The Organization's Website

Most organizations today have a website. Plan to include yours in the publicity campaign. Before you develop your message, go to the website and look at information that currently exists. A little research like this can get your mind in motion and trigger some ideas. Then, look for the webmaster's contact information and make contact. The webmaster will provide the information that you need to proceed. He or she should also be able to offer suggestions that will make your ad noticeable.

Prior to submitting your information, be sure to get another pair of eyes to look at it to make sure it accurately depicts your message. Also, provide the webmaster with dates on which you want your information published. Some suggested time frames are discussed later in this chapter.

The website is dynamic, meaning that it can be updated easily, but not necessarily at the last minute. So, check into the amount of time in which a change can take place and plan accordingly. This is a great method for keeping people up to date on the latest breaking news about your event and new auction items. You may also be able to send digital pictures of the items to create additional interest.

Word-of-Mouth

Sometimes word-of-mouth advertising is undervalued, though it can be one of the most successful approaches to use. People in your organization will tell others about the event, if they are reminded to and they are excited about it. The publicity committee is responsible for the reminders and creating excitement. People who are involved in the event will be your front runners in getting the word out. Here's a great analogy of what we are talking about.

Several years ago, there was a television commercial about shampoo. In the first scene, a woman was talking about how much she loved the shampoo and what it did for her. She said that she told two friends, who told two friends and so on and so on. Eventually, the television screen was filled with many faces of women who all loved the shampoo. The same applies when disseminating good news. Keep your volunteers motivated and excited and they'll tell two friends, who'll tell two friends, and so on.

There's More to the Story

In addition to getting the information out about the particulars of the event, you'll also want to make sure that your publicity includes the following:

- the organization's name and the event name
- the purpose of the event – include specifics on how the money will be used if you have the information, i.e. playground equipment
- the day, date and time that the event takes place
- the name, address and phone number of the venue
- request for additional auction items
- request for additional advertisers and underwriters
- volunteer opportunities
- ticket price

Now that you've had some time to think about what is involved with publicity, it's time to begin planning. Here are some guidelines to follow regarding the timing of certain types of publicity.

Timing	Message	Method
5 to 6 months prior to the event	SAVE THE DATE!	Verbal announcements, flyers, newsletter, website
2 to 4 months prior to the event	THE EVENT IS COMING!	Combination of verbal announcements, flyers, newsletter, website
6 weeks prior to the event	IT IS ALMOST HERE!	Posters – list of donated items to date
1 month prior to the event and each following week	General excitement and publicize auction items	Flyers, verbal announcements, website

As you plan, be creative with your thinking. Here are some additional ways to publicize events sponsored by schools and churches that are a lot of fun and very successful.

- Send flyers home with students in their backpacks on a regular basis with a list of items.
- Dress in themed clothing that represents the event and stand in the carpool line to sell tickets or give out flyers.
- Decorate your organization's main entrance using the event theme as a guide to generate interest among visitors.
- Ask the teachers for wear themed clothing on a specified day of the week to promote the event.
- Ask students to wear themed clothing on a specified day. Give a prize for the best dressed class.
- Print and sell themed T-shirts. Organization members can wear them in the days leading up to the event and you make a little more money!

Any combination of these ideas will generate an interest in your event and cause people to ask questions, get involved and look forward to attending.

Chapter 10

Who is gonna just GIVE US stuff?

Getting Donations

LOTS of people. Willingly. But they won't call YOU. Securing donations for the silent and live auctions as well as funds to assist in the production of the event is a significant effort. Your success in this area is the key to the amount of funds that you will raise. While not difficult, it does take planning, organization, contacting a large number of potential donors and good documentation.

There are several key steps in this process. They include the following:

- create a common purpose
- identify potential donors
- assign solicitation responsibilities
- prepare a solicitation letter
- contact potential donors for each item
- complete donor form
- document results
- collect funds/items
- log funds/item
- deposit funds/store items
- process donor forms
- write thank-you letters

Don't panic yet.   Each of these steps are discussed in detail throughout this chapter.

Create a Common Purpose

Every person involved in soliciting donations should be prepared to articulate the purpose of the event. Distribute a one or two sentence statement that describes what you want to accomplish so that there is a consistent message going out into the community. Here's a sample message:

"The playground equipment at Austin Elementary School is in need of repair so that our children can continue to play safely. We are raising money to replace all of the swings and add a new merry-go-round."

Identify Donors

First of all, this is not a one-person job! Involve as many people as you can. As a rule of thumb, everyone involved in the event should be responsible for soliciting donations in one way or another.   The designated committee members' key responsibilities are to solicit donations as well as pick them up, so even those who are uncomfortable asking for donations will have a job.

One way to start is to develop a list of items you would like to have donated based upon the target audience of the event. Then make a list of potential donors. You may have the luxury of having the list of donors from a previous event, however, if not, develop ideas by brainstorming. Ask your volunteers who have attended a recent auction to list items that they remember and if possible, give you a copy of the program!

Here are a few ideas to jump-start your thinking:

- gift certificates – restaurants, stores, golf course, internet shopping sites, beauty salons, cooking classes, etc.,
- tickets – football, baseball, tennis, basketball, tournaments, movies, museum, etc.,
- golf outings,
- airline tickets, frequent flyer miles, hotel stays
- gift baskets,
- services – personal, auto, car wash, maid, catering, flight lessons, tutoring, sports camps, babysitting, etc.,

- get-a-way trip – beach house, ski resort lodging, vacation home, etc
- art,
- craft items – let your imagination be your guide,
- photography - portrait session, fun camera for kids of all ages, etc.,
- holiday items – crafts, tablecloth and napkins, pottery, cards, stationery, etc.,
- children items – games, toys, books, playhouse, play gym, etc.,
- puppy, kitten, other small animals,
- performing arts – tickets to symphony, theater, opera, etc.,
- children outings – children's museum, zoo, butterfly museum, birthday party events, etc.,
- gourmet dinners for groups ,
- guest accommodations – hotels and bed and breakfast inns,
- short distance trip items – if you are within driving distance of a nice city to visit, put a package together to include a restaurant gift certificate, event tickets, housing accommodations, etc.,
- car rentals,
- home furnishings ,
- autographed items – cd's, pictures, sports memorabilia, books, etc.,
- ladies night out party at someone's home,
- progressive dinner for couples,
- crawfish boil for a large crowd,
- teachers and principals to donate outings or dinners,
- themed happy hours, brunches, luncheons,
- hot air balloon rides,
- group projects.

Want a little more to think about?!   Get creative. Look at the boxes your children's birthday gifts come in. Many times there are business addresses AND PHONE NUBMERS right on the box.

The Internet is another wonderful resource for ideas. Get your volunteers to surf the web and look for auctions that other organizations have had. Oftentimes, there is a list of donated items available that is just a mouse-click away! In addition, there are companies on the web that have sports memorabilia from famous athletes that is available to purchase and auction at a higher price. To find these companies, just go to the web and enter the word "auction" and you'll see links to websites with these offerings.

During our search we collected ideas from people with great experiences in this area. One person, in particular, successfully raised $100,000 as a result of their event. When asked about the types of donated items that were extremely successful, she said that dinners seemed most popular and brought in a lot of money.

Here is how that worked:

Groups of couples create a fun themed dinner party, cocktail party, etc. and open the bidding to a certain number of people at a specified cost. On the night of the Silent Auction every guest that placed their name on the list attends the party. Let's say that the cost for each person is $50 and the party accommodates 20 people. That is $1000 right there. Get as many of these as you can and watch the money flow!!

Keep Track as You Go!

To track all of your prospective donors, ask a volunteer with data entry skills to create a digital database. Here are the columns that you need in your database:

- company name
- contact
- title
- address
- address 2
- city
- state
- zip
- phone
- fax
- email
- website
- item requested/donated

This database will be used throughout the prospecting process. It can also be used to document results as discussed at the end of this chapter. And, of course, a template database is available for a free download at www.storymasterpress.com/auctionhelp

Assign Solicitation Responsibilities

Once you have a good working list, assign specific prospects to each volunteer to avoid duplication of effort.

The chairperson for this committee should maintain the master list for follow up with their committee members. They will want to touch base on a regular basis to make certain things are going well and to keep them motivated.

You may want to put an incentive program together that awards a prize for individual(s) who bring in the largest valued item, the most creative item and/or largest number of donated items. Here are some prize ideas:

- $25 cash
- Starbucks card
- gift certificate
- designated donation item
- frequent flyer miles - most airlines allow frequent flyers to "gift" their mileage points
- pre-paid gift catalogues

Regardless, of the prize, people love to win!

Prepare a Solicitation Letter

Before you begin soliciting for donations, prepare a letter that includes the purpose of the event, the request for the donation and the benefits to the donor. Provide each volunteer with a digital copy of the letter so that they can personalize it to the donor. Here is a sample letter:

Dear Hank:

The Miller Playhouse Booster Club, a parent-run group of volunteers, will be hosting a gala and auction to raise funds for the coming year. Our goal is to raise enough funds to purchase new seats and a new sound system for our theater.

Our gala will be held at ABC Restaurant, 1600 Restaurant Avenue , on Saturday, January 24, 2004, with all monies raised benefiting the Miller High School Playhouse. We hope that you will consider donating an auction item, gift certificate or gift basket to our silent auction. As a donor, you will receive publicity prior to and during the event, which will be viewed by every invitee and attendee. We will be sending over 300 invitations and expect to have 150 attendees.

May we count on your help? An auction committee member would be happy to pick up your item at your convenience, or if you would prefer, you may send it to Jane Doe, 631 Maple Drive, Houston TX 77002. Please submit your donation no later than January 10th to ensure proper recognition at the gala.

Thank you for your support of the Miller High School Playhouse, education and the arts.

Sincerely,

If you would like to have a digital copy of this letter, you may download it free at www.storymasterpress.com/auctionhelp.

Contact Potential Donors

Now you are ready to contact prospective donors. There are three types of donors – businesses, personal donations and underwriters for the event. We'll discuss each one of these separately.

Business Donations

Getting donations is overwhelming at times, but most businesses are willing to give donations for a good cause. In fact, every single business is a prospect. However, besides the "warm fuzzy feeling" they'll get by donating, there needs to be a good business reason as well.

So, how will businesses benefit from donating auction items? There are many benefits. Here are a few.

- association with your organization shows community support and is good for public relations
- provides the business an opportunity to advertise their products or services to a large number of people
- gives the business an opportunity to "get out of the box" and showcase their products and services in a different venue
- many companies have budgets from which they need to disperse charitable funds – donations are a great way to accomplish this
- donations are used by businesses as a tax write-off

As you begin soliciting donations, use these benefits as selling points to the prospective donors.

So, how do you go about doing this? There are three types of solicitation – correspondence, telephone, and face to face. Each is discussed below.

Correspondence

You've written your basic solicitation letter, now it is time to customize it for the business. The customization can be done through a mail merge process between your database and word-processing software like Microsoft Word. As you are customizing the letter, ask for a specific item that you need. This helps the donor focus on what to donate. Include the auction donor form as an attachment to the letter.

Plan to place a phone call to follow up on the letters that you send within 2 weeks from the date of the letter. Say something like this:

Hello Jim. My name is Sarah and I represent Austin Elementary School. I recently sent a letter to you regarding our upcoming auction. Have you had an opportunity to review it?

If the answer is "Yes," then say *"Great! Are you able to assist us with a donation?"*

If that answer is "Yes," then say, *"Thank you so much! Would you please complete the donation form and send it to me at.....?"*

If the answer is "No," then say, *"Thank you for considering our request. We have our auction every year. May we contact you next year?"*

Regardless of the response, you want to leave a good impression on the person to whom you were speaking. Who knows, maybe he or she will be in a position to donate something for next year's event.

Telephone Contact

It's been our experience that not everyone is comfortable soliciting donations over the phone, so here are some tips for your success:

When placing the call ask for a specific person. If you don't have a contact name, ask to speak to the owner, the manager or the person responsible for charitable donations.

Next, use a script and practice until it feels easy. The first time you do this will be the most difficult. However, the remaining contacts will become easier.

The script should contain these key elements. First, the person you are contacting needs to know who you are and the purpose of your call. Next, discuss the organization and the purpose of the event. Finally, ask for the donation. Here's a sample script:

> *"Good morning, my name is Linda Johnson. May I speak to the person responsible for charitable donations?"*
>
> *"Ms. Smith, thanks for taking my call (or seeing me if in person). I represent XYZ School located in west Houston. We are holding a fund-raising event in September to build a new playground. We expect approximately 900 people to attend, giving your business an opportunity to for great exposure.*
>
> *"What would you be willing to donate something to our event?"*

Once you have gone through the script to this point, the prospect is engaged. Be prepared with the types of items you would like to have donated. For example, if you are speaking to a dry cleaner, ask for a gift certificate for dry cleaning. When speaking to a sporting goods store, ask for camping equipment or a bicycle. The key here is to be specific about your needs.

Face to Face Contact

Making contacts in person involves walking into a business and asking to speak to the person responsible for making charitable donations. Typically, this type of contact is the most successful. Take generic solicitation letters and donor forms with you so that you can provide them to the decision maker immediately. Dress in a business casual manner and greet your contact with a handshake, good eye contact and a smile.

When making the call remember that the person to whom you are speaking is busy running the business and will only have a few minutes to share. Be succinct and get to the point quickly.

Personal Donations

These donations can be a simple as buying a lamp and donating it and as elaborate as a week's stay in a French chateau. The best way to get donations in this manner is to tell everyone about the event. You may also publish a list of desired items in the organization's newsletter or through email, etc. Most people are willing to donate something or go in with others to do so.

Ruth chaired an Auction and Spaghetti Dinner to raise funds for sending the youth choir to Europe. Because each child directly benefited from the funds raised, each family was asked to donate something to the auction, bring a dessert for the spaghetti dinner, and each child signed up for a service to auction – such as babysitting. These personal donations were a huge hit and raised a lot of money.

Underwriting

The third group of prospective donors consists of businesses and individuals who are interested in underwriting a portion of the expenses incurred in putting on the event. They are referred to as either underwriters or sponsors. The key difference here is that they may donate money towards a specific purpose such as the invitations, decorations or they may donate money to the general event versus donating a product or service that will be purchased by the attendees. One chairperson told us that they raised $30,000 in underwriting dollars based on specific giving levels that correlated to tables at the event. For example, a $5,000 donation was considered a Platinum Sponsorship, $2,000 a Gold Sponsorship, and so on.

There are many opportunities for underwriters with an event. You'll provide them with options on how their dollars can be spent. Here are some examples:

- table decorations
- printing of programs and invitations
- live auctioneer
- music for the event
- publicity signage

You may need to use general terms about your needs and ask for a specific minimum amount such as $100.

Some underwriters may request that their dollars be used to purchase banners for the event. Typically, they want their name on the banner. This works well because it creates publicity for the donor and the event.

You may choose to create different levels of underwriting based upon dollar amounts donated. For example, you may have a silver category for $100, a gold category for $200 and a platinum category for $300. Use your theme as a guide for the names of the donor levels.

A rule of thumb is that underwriters are guaranteed recognition in the program. Another thing we recommend is to use donated dollar amounts to create seating arrangements. The donor who contributes the largest dollar amount sits at the front center table and you work out from there. If you do not have a specified seating arrangement it is still a good idea to reserve the best table for your highest underwriter.

Underwriters are often solicited through written correspondence, but most big underwriting gifts are the result of personal connections and face-to-face contact. Therefore, if the organization feels large amounts can be raised in this way, it is important for the Underwriting Chairperson to be well connected, and be proficient in asking for those kinds of donations.

Each business prospect will have someone in their organization that is responsible for charitable donations. Assign the collection of names for your mailing list to volunteers on the Ads and Underwriting Committee. A simple phone call to the business asking for the name of the person responsible for charitable donations is the most effective way to build your list. Addressing letters to specific individuals is preferable, however, a letter addressed to "Attention: Charitable Donations" may also get results.

When writing your correspondence, be sure to include the specific purpose for the request. Here's a sample letter:

December 5, 2003

Dear [Underwriter Sponsor], (*Note: fill in name before sending!!*)

American Middle School is pleased to announce the 2004 auction, "*Wild, Wild, West .*" On February 6th we will celebrate the many accomplishments of our middle school while raising funds to enhance and maintain the high standards of our programs.

We invite your business to participate as an underwriter. There are many levels to choose from and we can work with your company's payment schedule.

School needs at this time include classroom upgrades such as additional reading, math and science interactive software, class sets of English books, new atlases directed toward world culture studies, math manipulatives used in math tutorials, and student recognition for attendance, academics and conduct. We are also seeking campus beautification in the areas of enhanced landscaping, outdoor seating and learning center, library artwork and motivational banners.

As you can see, we are a second-year school with many needs that are not met by the school budget. Your participation is needed. Please take a look at the attached donor form to select your giving level. Make an impact on the youth of our area today!

If you have questions, need help with a proposal or have an alternate suggestion, please give us a call.

Sincerely,

When planning your underwriting solicitation campaign, you may want to group the same types of businesses together such as realtors or banks. The purpose of this approach is to create a desire on the part of each business to say "I need to donate, too." Set the dollar amount at something that is reasonable and that will not cause a business to "blink". Here is a sample letter sent to realtors:

Realtor Round-Up
For
"WILD, WILD, WEST "
2003-2004 Auction Fundraiser
February 6, 2004
The Club, Houston, Texas

November 15, 2003

Dear Sponsor,

American Middle School is please to announce the 2004 auction, "**WILD, WILD, WEST.'** On February 6th we will celebrate the many accomplishments of our middle school while raising funds to enhance and maintain the high standards of our programs.

We are asking all realtors in our area to make a commitment to American. You may choose from one of many levels detailed on the next page or participate in the **Realtor's Round-Up. Join your peers in pledging $100 or more per company.** The realty company with the largest pledge will have the opportunity to provide your choice of a logo item such as notepads, calendars or magnets (pens have been assigned).

School needs at this time include campus beautification, classroom upgrades such as additional reading, math and science interactive software, class sets of English books, new atlases directed toward world culture studies, math manipulatives used in math tutorials, and student recognition for attendance, academics and conduct.

Make an impact on the youth of our area today! If you have questions, need help with a proposal or have an alternate suggestion, please give us a call.

Sincerely,

Along with the letter, send an underwriter's donor form so that it is easy for them to reply to your request. Here is a sample form.

Underwriter's Donor Form
WILD, WILD, WEST
2003-2004 Auction Fundraiser
February 6, 2004
The Club, Houston, Texas

_____ Yes, I will participate as an underwriter!

Contact Name_____
Business Name_____
Address_____City_____State_____Zip_____
Phone_____Fax_____eMail_____

All donors at the following levels will receive mention in the program catalog, signage at the event newsletter mention and a framed thank you letter.

__ Banners/Event Posters	Western Union Level	$500
__ Flowers	Desert Cactus Level	$350

Sponsor
__ Platinum $300
__ Gold $200
__ Silver $100

__ I cannot utilize funds until later into 2004, and will send underwriting funds on or before March 15, 2004 (mark the amount above).

__ Charge my underwriting funds to the following credit card account:
List name and card number_____ Exp. Date___

Items will also be accepted in lieu of underwriting.

Your response is appreciated by January 30, 2004.

Mail to: _PTO_, c/o Chairperson, Address, Houston, Texas, Zip

---

Go to www.storymasterpress.com/auctionhelp to download these sample forms.

Before we move on to donor forms – here's a quick note about correspondence - We have all been taught at an early age not to judge a book by its cover, but we all do. This said, businesses will judge your organization by the way the letter looks. There are several important things to consider when sending correspondence.

First, all correspondence should be on the organization's letterhead or stationery with the organization's logo. This gives a formal and professional look to your letter.

Second, make sure that you use proper grammar and proofread for correct spelling.

Third, make certain that the reader knows who to contact for any questions by putting the name, title, and contact information. Be sure to include an email address. If the organization has a website, include that as well.

Complete Item Donor Forms

When the prospective donor says "Yes!" be sure to pat yourself on the back for a job well done and provide the donor with a donation form to complete. It's best to have the donor complete the form because they may have a specific way in which they want their item and business represented.

Donor forms should be printed in triplicate to make the process easier. Make certain that your donor form includes the following:

- name of the event and date
- donor name, address, telephone and email
- description of the auction item
- fair market value of the item
- explanation of use of the item - such as expiration date, times, etc.
- date
- signature of donor
- organization contact information

Finally, the donor form should be printed with the event name, organization name and logo.

A sample form is located on the next page.

If you would like to have a digital copy of this form, you may download it free at www.storymasterpress.com/auctionhelp.

The USA High School Booster Club Gala
Auction Donation Form
January 24, 2004

Name: _____

Business: _____

Address   : _____

Name as you want it in the program: _____

Phone: Work: _____   Home: _____

Email: _____

Description
of auction item :

_____

_____

_____

_____

Fair Market Value: $_____

Donor's Signature _____

Date   _____

Contact Jane Doe at 281-531-8888 or jdoe@aol.com with any questions.

Please return this form to:
USA High School Booster Club
P.O. Box 1234
Houston TX 77002

Received by: _____

Collect and Store Items and Deposit Funds

Collecting donated items such as gift certificates and checks is often done through the mail. However, in many instances, the items will need to be picked up. As a courtesy to the donor, arrange to have the item picked up at a convenient time. Make arrangements for storage of the collected items early on in the process and publish the location to all committee members so that anyone collecting items will know where to take them prior to the event.

When a check is received, it should go to the Treasurer of the event for deposit immediately.

Document Results

Documentation is critical in the donation process. First of all, you need to be able to stay on top of the solicitation activity and results. Second, you'll need to forward the list to the Publicity Chairman for use in promoting the event and third, you'll need the information for writing thank you notes. Finally, the list will be used for the next year's event.

Earlier in this chapter we mentioned creating a digital database of prospective donors. That database can be copied and columns added for the final documentation.

Digital documentation is accomplished through the use of software. There is software available on the market today that is specifically designed for use with auctions. We discuss the benefits of utilizing this type of software in Chapter 3.

If you do not have this software, don't worry, you can use either a spreadsheet software like Microsoft Excel or word processing software like Microsoft Word. We recommend using Excel because it has the ability to total dollar amounts automatically.

Regardless of the tool that you use, your documentation should include the following columns:

- donor's name
- donor's address and phone
- donor's email address
- item category
- item description
- item number
- item value
- special notes
- winning bid amount
- winning bidder, address, phone and email
- total funds raised

This documentation is done in three phases. The first phase is done as you collect donor forms. Log each item onto the spreadsheet and assign a category and a tracking number. The second phase is done when all of your items have been collected. At this point, you'll assign numbers to each. The final phase of documentation occurs after the auction. We discuss this in chapter 14.

Process Donor Forms

We recommend the donor form be printed on a three part, self copying forms. When the item is received and logged in, the original should be attached to the item and the other two parts of the form go to the donor and the appropriate live or silent auction chairperson. The form is then held until the day of the event at which time the remaining copies will be dispersed. More on that in Chapter 14.

Write Thank You Letters

This step is very important in the process and must not be overlooked. Each donor should receive a thank-you letter on your organization's letterhead. There are a couple of schools of thought on when to send the letter. You may choose to send the letter as soon as you receive the item to keep the task from becoming overwhelming. Or, you may wait until the event is over so that you can include the amount of funds raised. It is important to be very prompt with your letters. Set a goal to have them out within 48 hours of the event. Consider having recipients of the funds write the letters. One year we had students werite the thank-you's (each student was given one person to thank). The donors were THRILLED and some even KEPT the letters.

Here is a sample thank-you letter:

Dear Mr. Smith:

Thank you so much for your recent contribution to the USA Singers Fundraiser. Your donation of $500 was most generous and greatly appreciated. Proceeds from the fundraiser will be used to help underwrite the choir's upcoming trip to England in March. The singers are very excited and your generous donation will help raise the funds needed to put the cost of the trip within reach of our group.

All donations are tax-deductible within the limits specified by law and our records reflect that you received no goods or services in return for your donation. USA Singers is a tax-exempt organization under section 501 (c)(3) of The Internal Revenue Code.

On behalf of the choir, parents and staff of USA Singers, please accept our thanks for your wonderful support.

Sincerely,

Ready, Get Set, Go!!!

Before you get started, here are just a few final tips. Start early. Get lots of volunteers. Put a great list of ideas together for donations. Consider everyone you know as a prospective donor or referral for a donor. Remember, the worst thing someone can tell you is "No" and so far, we haven't found that to be fatal. And finally, HAVE FUN!

Chapter 11

Think ya'll can make it???

Invitations and Reservations

Invitations

In addition to all your other publicity, the invitation is probably the most important promotion tool you have. To be successful, make certain that your invitation list has been given a lot of thought. Here are some things to consider when making your list:

- Determine the number of people to invite by considering
  o the size of the venue
  o how many people you want to attend, and
  o printing and mailing costs.
- Use the previous year's mailing list as a guide and add additional names by brainstorming with committee members. Here are some other ideas:
  o Add all new members of the organization to the list.
  o Consider other possible attendees such as:
    ▪ family members,
    ▪ the organization's dignitaries,
    ▪ city officials, and
    ▪ the organization's board of directors.

- o If you are planning an event for a school, invite the
  - ▪ principals of district-wide schools that feed students into your school,
  - ▪ all teachers and school staff, and
  - ▪ the district superintendent and high ranking staff.

As you review your list, highlight the names of former attendees who were your highest bidders and follow up to make sure that they receive their invitations.

Your mailing list should be in a digital format. If you do not have auction software, Microsoft Excel is a good choice because it can sort the data in many ways. Here is a sample format for you to follow:

Event Mailing List

Last Name	First Name	Street Address	City	State	Zip	Phone	Reserv. Rec'd
Smith	John	1234 Apple	Park	TX	77001	XXX-XXXX	

If you'd like a digital copy of this form, go to
www.storymasterpress.com/auctionhelp for a free download.

Designing the Invitation

Creating the invitation is so much fun! Using the theme of the event as your guide, generate ideas that are a little out of the box. What we mean here is that you want your invitation to "jump out" as the recipient opens the envelope. In addition to being eye-catching, the invitation should include the following:

- organization's name & the event name
- purpose of the event
- attire
- day, date and time of the event
- address and phone number of the venue
- cost per person
- reservation information and pre-payment due date
- levels of donation support – (donations are often made if the recipient can't attend)
- honoree (if applicable)
- major underwriters

Here are some invitation ideas that may give you some inspiration!

Theme	Invitation Idea
A Taste of the Orient	Use small Chinese "take out" boxes. Print the invitation and place it on the outside. Put a fortune cookie inside for fun!
50's Era	Old 45 records make terrific invitations! Print the invitation and place it in the center of the record.
Nautical	Create the invitation in the form of a passport. You may want to put a phase like "Your Passport To A Wonderful Evening" on the front and print the invitation on the inside.
Parisian Nights	Nothing says "Paris" like the Eiffel Tower!

Designing the Reservation Card

In addition to the invitation, you will be designing a reservation card. The information on the card will vary based upon the type of seating that you are planning.

Some events do not require seating assignments. Typically, this occurs when you are just serving hors d'oeuvres and cocktails.

You may choose to have a buffet and offer first come first served seating. If you choose this option, make seating cards that have the guests names on them. On the night of the event, you can place them at the check-in table and your guests can select their seating and place their name card at their seat. If you choose this approach, make certain that it is clear on the invitation.

A general reservation card will work just fine for unassigned seating. Here's a sample:

Reservation Card 1 – No assigned seating

Event Name Reservation

Guest Name(s)_____

_____

_____

_____

Number of guests attending _____

Any special accommodations? _____

Contact Phone Number _____

I cannot attend, but please accept my donation of $_____

Payment Information:

Check enclosed in the amount of $_____

Credit Card Number _____

Expiration Date _____

If you choose to make seating assignments, this card will do:

Reservation Card 2 – Assigned Seating

Event Name Reservation

Guest Name(s)_____   _____
                 _____   _____
                 _____   _____
                 _____   _____
                 _____   _____

Please reserve a table in the name of _____

Any special accommodations? _____

Contact Phone Number _____

I cannot attend, but please accept my donation of $_____

Payment Information:

Check enclosed in the amount of $_____

Credit Card Number _____

Expiration Date _____

Another option for reservations involves purchasing tables at sponsor levels. In some instances, tables are given different price ranges based upon where they are located in the room. This applies mainly if there is entertainment and a live auction. For example, a $10,000 table is front and center, surrounding tables may be $8,000 and all others $5,000. The purpose for this is to give large donors priority seating.

This type of seating requires a reservation card and some additional planning regarding table reservations. Here is a sample reservation card:

Reservation Card 3 – Sponsor Reserved/General Seating

Event Name Reservation

Guest Name(s)_____   _____

_____   _____

_____   _____

_____   _____

_____   _____

Please reserve the following type of table in the name of _____

Any special accommodations? _____

O **$10,000 Sponsor**   O **$8,000 Sponsor**   O **$5,000 Table** O **General Seating**

Contact Phone Number _____

I cannot attend, but please accept my donation of $_____

Payment Information:

Check enclosed in the amount of $_____

Credit Card Number _____

Expiration Date _____

Accepted Forms of Payment

You'll notice that a credit card number line is on each of the reservation cards. Prior to designing the reservation cards, you'll need to determine what forms of payment will be acceptable. There are a couple of things to consider as you make your decision.

If you choose to accept cash, check and credit cards, you need to be prepared for each. When credit cards are accepted, you need to factor in the percentage of the sale that is paid to the credit card company for the use of their card. In addition, you need to have a merchant's account set up, typically through your organization's bank, so that you can accept credit payments. While this may seem a little overwhelming, people tend to spend more when they can use a credit card.

If you choose to accept cash and checks only, make certain that you note this information on the reservation card and ask your check-in committee to make a sign for the check-in table to avoid any questions.

Online Reservations

In the high-tech world in which we live, we are presented with opportunities to reduce expenses. Using your organization or event's website, create an online reservation process for your guests to use. This method is inexpensive, available 24/7 and it eliminates mailing time.

This is a valuable add-on to the page on the organization's website devoted to the event. If the organization's website can't accommodate you, consider creating a web page just for the event. There are many companies with whom you can work to develop your web page. If you need any guidance in this area, go to www.storymasterpress.com and click on the Website help link.

The Reservations Chairperson along with the Publicity Chairperson should spearhead this project. Be sure to include the online reservation option on the invitation.

One Final Thought about Invitations

Invitations can be elaborate or simple. When making your decision, consider the impact the invitation will have on the recipient and the overall cost of printing and postage.

Preparing the Reservations List

As you begin receiving guest reservations, enter the names into your database to build your guest list. Take care to spell names correctly, because you will be using this list to create name tags. If you are unsure, place a call to the number on the reservation card to get the correct spelling.

After you enter the guests' names on your list, assign one bidder number beside each. (NOTE: Couples receive ONE bidder number.) This bidder number will be used by the Check-In Committee as they assemble the check-in packets. The numbers will also be used for check out, so make certain there aren't any duplicate numbers. You may choose to start with 100 as your first number and go from there.

When your list is complete, you will give it to the Check-In Committee Chairperson to use to check guests off as they arrive.

Chapter 12

Program? Why don't we just tell people where to go and what to do?

The Event Program

The program for the event is an important tool for your guests. It contains the evening's activities and a catalogue of all the items that are available in both the Silent and the Live Auctions. You may choose to cover the cost of printing a nice glossy program by asking local businesses if they would like to purchase advertising space.

If you choose to offer advertising opportunities, you should approach this as diligently as you do getting donations for auction items. Here's how you get started:

Create Ad Space Sizes and Costs

The first step in this process is to determine the size of the program. Most programs are 8 ½" x 11" but you may wish to consider an 5 ½" x 8 ½" sized program to reduce cost. Once you've decided the size of the program the next step is to create ad space.

Most of the time ads are offered in these sizes – business card size, ¼ page, ½ page, full page, inside front page and inside back page and back cover. The costs for these ads increase as the size increases. For example, a business card sized ad could cost $80, a ¼ page ad could cost $100, a ½ page ad - $200 and so on. The best way to determine pricing is to ask some people you know who place ads like this for some average costs and go from there.

Compose an Ad Patron Letter

Create a letter that requests support for your organization through advertising. Businesses may be approached either through personal contact or through the mail. Regardless, it is important to have a letter that details the advertising opportunities that are available. Also create an Ad Order Form to attach to the letter so that ad patrons can place their orders easily.

Here is a sample letter and ad order form:

Dear Ad Patron:

Our organization is hosting a fundraising event in January. The purpose of this event is to raise funds to replace the computer equipment in the computer lab. Currently our students are sharing computers and we look forward to the day that each student will have access to a computer simultaneously.

Our event will include both a silent and live auction and we expect to have 200 – 300 people attend. The purpose of this letter is to offer your business an opportunity to be showcased via advertising in our program for the evening.

We have enclosed an Ad Order Form with the sizes and costs of the available advertising space. We appreciate your consideration and look forward to advertising your business.

Sincerely,

---

142 Ruth McCurdy & Linda Oppenheim

Ad Order Form

Business Name _____

Contact Name _____

Address _____

Phone Number _____Email_____

Select ad size below:

o Business Card @ $80
   (3.75" w x 2.5" h)
o ¼ page @ $180
   (4.25" w x 5.5" h)
o 1/2 page @ $280
   (8.5" w 5.5" h)

Circle one: Hard copy enclosed; CD ROM/Diskette enclosed;
             Will email ad to rusty@aol.com

Payment amount: _____Cash _____Check #_____Date Rec'd

Business contact signature _____

Ad Deadline: 8/13/04

Once the ad order forms start coming in, someone needs to work with the printer to design the layout of the ads. It's a good idea to find out how the printer's process works prior to soliciting for ads so that you know deadlines that must be kept. When the ads are ready to go, you should send them to the business contact via email to make certain that they look just right and get final approval.

Personal Ads

In addition to business ads, you may want to solicit personal ads (no not that kind!) to recognize teachers, groups for achievements, etc. Let's use a school program for example. One idea may be an ad that thanks a teacher and it is signed by students. Another idea is to congratulate a team for winning district. There are many ideas to run with, so you may want to designate the solicitation of personal ads to several volunteers.

Program Design

While the ad process is in full swing, someone can be typing the program. It's important to assign someone to this task that either has experience or that is meticulous and pays strict attention to details. Also assign other volunteers to participate in proofing the program before it goes to print. The cover reflects the theme of the event. Be creative and have fun with it.

Program Contents

The event program is really based upon the amount of information that you want to put into your guests hands. Here are some ideas for you to consider:

- the name, date and location of the event
- a letter from a senior ranking official in the organization thanking the attendees and donors for their participation
- the menu
- the program – specific activities and times for each
- a list of underwriters organized by amount donated
- the organization's mission statement, if applicable
- the organization's board of directors
- the auction committee chairpersons and committee members
- a list of donors in alphabetical order
- auction rules and procedures
- donated items, along with the donor's name and a description of each item up for bid
- business and personal ads

As mentioned earlier, the size and content of your program will be based upon the amount of information you want to put into your guests hands as well as the associated cost of the program. At a minimum, we suggest that you include the following:

- the name, date and location of the event
- thank-you page for the event committee persons and underwriters
- the program listing the activities and times for each
- a list of items donated along with the donor's name and the fair market value of the donation (FMV)
- auction rules and procedures

Auction Rules and Procedures

The purpose of listing the auction rules and procedures is to reduce the risk of guests being confused about what to expect with the auction and to eliminate any hard feelings that could occur. On the next page we've listed some sample auction rules and procedures for you to consider as you plan your program.

Auction Rules and Procedures

General Rules

- All sales are final. No exchanges or refunds permitted.

- Gift certificates are not redeemable for cash.

- All items are sold "as is". The item description is as accurate as possible and the committee is not responsible for any discrepancies that may occur.

- The decisions of the auctioneer and the committee are final.

- Reservations for dinners, use of homes, trips, etc. must be mutually arranged with the donor, unless otherwise specified. All accommodations and travel are subject to availability and donor restrictions.

- Some items have expiration and black out dates. If not specified, offers and items expire one year from date of issue.

- Read your gift certificate carefully!

- Group bidding is welcome and is an excellent way to join together and share many of the larger items. However, one person must take responsibility for the bidding and for notifying auction officials as to the names of all buyers.

Check-In Procedures

- A bidder packet including a live auction bid sign and bidder number will be given to each couple or individual attending the event as they check in.

- The packet will include a table assignment number and name tags for each guest.

- Final auction bids constitute a binding agreement to pay for purchases.

Live Auction Rules

- Professional auctioneer, (auctioneer's name) will conduct the live auction.

- To enter a bid, the bidder will raise his or her bid sign directing a signal to the auctioneer or one of the spotters.

- The highest bidder acknowledged by the auctioneer shall be the buyer.

- In the event of a dispute, the auctioneer shall have the sole and final decision to determine the successful bidder or to re-offer and resell the item in dispute.

- High bidders will give their name and number to the spotter at the conclusion of bidding for each item.

- Payment by the successful bidder may be made at the check-out station before acquiring the item. Payment may be made by cash, check or credit card.

- High bidders should pick up their items in the auction check-out room before leaving at the end of the evening.

- Payment in full is mandatory prior to the end of the evening.

Silent Auction Rules

- The silent auction will run from 7:00 P.M. until 9:30 P.M. The Gold Table closing will follow.

- The last bidder and highest bid on a silent auction item bid sheet will win the purchase of that item.

- Your signature on the bid sheet signifies your agreement to pay.

- Each item will have its own bid sheet.

- A minimum opening bid and minimum raise amount will appear on each bid sheet.

- You may bid by placing your name on the first available uncovered space on a bid sheet.

- High bidders should pick up their silent auction items from the silent auction area after payment is made, and before leaving at the end of the evening.

Check-Out Procedures

- Check the Winners' Board for your name.

- Proceed to the check-out station to pay for your item(s).

- Following your payment at the end of the evening, you will proceed with your receipt to the silent auction area, where a volunteer will retrieve your item(s).

- The fair market value for each item is stated in the auction program.

- **PLEASE REMEMBER THAT YOU ARE RESPONSIBLE FOR TAKING YOUR ITEMS HOME TONIGHT. HELPERS ARE AVAILABLE IF YOU NEED ASSISTANCE TO YOUR CAR.**

As you can see, these rules and procedures are very straightforward. After you have written the rules and procedures for your event, ask several people who are not actively involved in the planning and preparation of the event to review them and give you any feedback they may have to help clarify any questions.

Typing the Program

Typing the program is a tedious, painstaking task requiring total accuracy. Make certain that the volunteers assigned to this project begin early and have LOTS of other eyes proofing the work.

This is one area where auction software can save a lot of time. For example, when donation descriptions are entered into the software to make the bid sheets, the software will use these descriptions to develop the program as well.

Regardless of your chosen approach, proofreading is critical. As you proof the program, pay specific attention to dates and days, times, and spelling of individuals' names.

Enforce deadlines to make sure that the program is ready in time. We recommend that the program be printed and ready to go one week prior to the event to ensure that it is ready. YES!!! There will be last minute donated items that won't make the program, but the majority will be there. If there is something that is missed and you must call attention to it, do so during the auction. An addendum can be added the night of the event for those items that come in after the printing of the program. These are NOT compromises to the program, but rather they are proof of the dynamic, ever-changing importance of the event!!

If you would like to see a sample program, go to
www.storymasterpress.com/auctionhelp.

And Awaaaaaay We Go

Chapter 13

Right this way—Just check your wallet here.

Guest Check-In

Preparation

When guests arrive, you want to make sure that they are greeted with warm, smiling faces and a smooth process. To accomplish this, you'll want to select volunteers who are outgoing and organized to man the check-in table. In addition, everything that will be needed for check-in should be prepared well in advance of the evening and double checked for accuracy. This is another place where an "unfamiliar" set of eyes may catch something you've overlooked since day one. We often use husbands for this task but ours are friendly and well trained. You use your own judgment.

Typically, guests receive a pre-assembled packet containing the following:

- name tags,
- live auction paddles,
- auction program/catalog,
- pens or pencils (optional),
- and their table assignments, if applicable.

Name Tags

To begin your preparation, get the list of reserved guests from the Reservations Chairperson to make your name tags. We suggest that you type the names of the guests and print them so they are easy to read.

The stock for name tags can be found in office supply stores and work with almost any printer.

Creating name tags may seem trivial, but when worn, they help "break the ice" when people meet for the first time. Put both the first and last name on the name tag. You may want to make the first name larger than the last and place it over the last name like so:

JANE **Doe**	**vs.**	**The Ducks In** **A Row Ball** *Jane Doe*

This makes the first name much easier to read. Also, remember, the function of a name tag is NOT to promote the event where the people already are – but rather to help folks know one another's NAMES. Sure you can be creative – but if you put logos or other "clutter" on the name tag for the eye to sort through be SURE that the NAME is the largest type! And be sure it is printed in a DEEPLY contrasting color to the background so it JUMPS off the tag. Snappy, clever name tags that are hard to read get an "F" for usefulness. This is a FUNCTION over FORM item.

In addition to preparing name tags for reserved guests, be prepared to have blank ones to use the night of the event for emergency use (in case a name is misspelled) and for walk-ins. If you do not plan to have a computer with printing capabilities at the check-in table, take a thick black marker with you to use. It is much easier to read than color.

Live Auction Paddles

As we mentioned earlier in Chapter 8, use your imagination to create the auction paddles. As you design your auction paddle, keep these thoughts in mind:

- It must be large enough to be seen by spotters, but small enough to fit into your auction packets.

- It must include a bidder number.

- And don't forget to make extra paddles to accommodate walk-in guests.

The Auction Program/Catalog

The design and printing of the program, also known as the catalog, is done by the Program Chairperson. Arrange to get the number of copies you need for reserved guests, typically one per person or per couple, and enough to have available for walk in guests.

Pens/Pencils

We listed this as an optional item for the check-in packets. You may choose to have pens or pencils imprinted with the event theme and date for your guests to have as a memento. If you choose not to include pens or pencils in the packets, make sure that you let the Silent Auction Chairperson know that they will be needed by the bid sheet at each auction item unless you are using bid stickers.

Assembling the Check-in Packets

This can be a fun job as well as an opportunity to get folks together. Form an assembly line and check each guest's name off the reservation list as you assemble their packet. As you are working, use this opportunity to do a final check to make sure that names are spelled correctly and that the paddles with bidder numbers are matched correctly to each guest. Write guests names on the outside of the packets and alphabetize. Divide the packets into alphabetical groups so that the process will move quickly.

Check-in Procedures

Plan your check-in procedures and then type and distribute to the folks who will be working at the check-in table. Make sure that all questions are answered and you will enjoy a smooth check-in process. Here are some sample procedures to follow:

- Welcome each guest enthusiastically!

- Ask the guest's name and check it against the reservation guest list.

- Give guests their packets and describe the contents

- Introduce them to volunteers assigned to give directions.

- Give guests an overview of the venue, what they will find and where

- Let guests know that there will be volunteers available in each area who can handle any questions they may have

- Wish guests a great evening!

Now, this process works perfectly, if there are no walk-ins. Determine early on in your planning process if you are able to take walk-ins. If you choose do to so, make certain that the venue can accommodate them with food and seating. In addition, you'll need to be prepared to accept their payment at the door. It can cost a bit more but, reserving an extra 4 to 8 meals can ensure some walk-in coverage. If your venue is flexible you may not have to make this financial commitment.

Because you have a guest reservation list, you will know immediately, by checking the list, if the guest does not have a reservation. When this occurs, follow these procedures:

- Write the guest's name down on your reservation list and assign them the next paddle number

- Create a name tag for the guest

- Give the guest one of the extra packets that you created

- Get their address and phone number if you don't have it already

Credit Card Processing

Another thought to consider in your check-in process is to ask each guest if he or she would like to pay for items won during the evening with a credit card. Ask if they would mind if you took an imprint of their card prior to their going into the event. The purpose here is to facilitate a quick check-out process. If the guest has any concerns, let them know that no charges will be made if they don't win any of the auction items. Most folks won't have a problem with this request, but if they do, just assure them that they can present their credit cards for payment at the end of the evening. After all, you are, "…just trying to get them home a bit earlier."

A Final Thought

The first impression of the event is made when a guest arrives at the check-in table. Your goal is to have them leave the area armed with information and filled with excitement for the evening!

Chapter 14

Shhh. We're the only bidders!

The Silent Auction

At this point, you have secured a large number of your items. Believe it or not, items come in the day of and sometimes even the evening of the auction! Often times a large number of items can come in during the week of the auction, so don't be discouraged if you don't have a huge number prior to that week.

The silent auction process consists of these steps.*

PRIOR TO:

1. Collect auction items and assign numbers
2. Provide auction item descriptions to Publicity Chairperson
3. Organize auction items
4. Prepare bid sheets
5. Prepare gift certificates

DAY OF:

6. Set up silent auction display
7. Open the auction
8. Monitor the auction
9. Close the auction
10. Alphabetize winners
11. Check-Out

* If you are using auction software, many of these steps will be automated.

Collect Auction Items and Assign Numbers

We've discussed the collection of auction items in Chapter 10. You will find specific details that will make your silent auction more successful.

The first step in organizing your auction items is to assign a number to them. The purpose of this number is to track each donation. An easy way to assign numbers is to begin with 100 followed by 101, 102, etc. Each item number should be documented alongside the name of the item on a spreadsheet. Then, write it on the donor form and attach the donor form to the item. See example.

Auction Donor Form

Name: _____

Business: _____

Address _____

_____

Phone -Work: _____ Home: _____

Email: _____

Description of auction item:

_____

_____

Value: $_____

Donor's Signature _____

Date   _____

Please return this form to Jane Doe by January 22, 2004

Thank you so much for your donation. We appreciate your support!

Auction Committee Only
Received by:_____ Category _____
p   Live Auction   Item # _____
p   Silent Auction   Opening Bid_____

Provide Auction Item Descriptions to Publicity Chairperson

One form of publicity is to promote the items that have been donated to generate excitement about the event. Make a list of items that would create a buzz and pass them on to the Publicity Chairperson. This should be done each week prior to the event. Start this process when you begin receiving donations.

Organize Auction Items

Select a location to store incoming auction items. Typically, a committee member may donate some space in his/her home, but in some instances, a storage facility may be needed. As the auction items arrive, place them in numerical order.

As you review the items, think about how you may want to group some of them as packages. This is important because single items may not captivate a buyer, but when grouped together generate a higher perceived value.

For example, dining gift certificates bundled with movie or event tickets are a great combination. A spa package and a lunch gift certificate is another idea. As you do this, put yourself in the shoes of the buyers and create combinations that will be hard to pass up! Be creative when naming the items. The more creative you are, the more interest you will generate. Right or wrong, books are judged by their covers. Why'd you buy this one?

Here are some other ideas:

- Junk Food Junkie or Fast Food Freak – a combination of fast food restaurant gift certificates

- Kids Day Out – Roller skating, putt putt golf, theme parks, zoo tickets

- Beach Blanket Bingo – a stay at a beach house complete with beach towels and water games

- Who Says You're a Wino?! - Wine Rack filled with wine bottles

- Oktoberfest??? - A cooler filled with beer

- Themed gift baskets are a great way to group different items

- Wanna Get Lucky? – A trip to the horse races (if available) or could be used for a romantic evening

- Bon Voyage – airline tickets with a cruise or a vacation home

Assembling packages is done after you have collected the majority of your items. The numbers for the individual items in the packages no longer apply. Assign a new number to the assembled packages and be sure to document the change on your spreadsheet.

Prepare Bid Sheets

The bid sheet is the document that is used for recording the bidding. The bid sheet includes the name and number of the item along with lines for individuals to use to bid. There are a couple of different types of bid sheets used in a silent auction.

Wish Lists

A Wish List is used when the organization wants to raise money for well-defined items such as playground equipment. This approach is well received as guests have an opportunity to fund something specific that is needed. Here is a sample of this type of form:

Wish List Bid Sheet

Children's Playground Equipment

Please place your name next to an item that you are willing

to purchase. We appreciate your support!

Item	Price	Name	Phone	Email
10 dodge balls	$75.00			
10 sets of knee pads	$100.00			
3 stop watches	$45.00			

Standard Bid Sheets

The "Standard" in bid sheet form is a page that features the item, a description and a minimum bid and raise amount along with a series of blanks for people to sign and print their bid. This form looks like this:

#100 Hail, Hail, The Gang's All Here!!

Description: 10 VIP Passes to Opening Night

Donor:　　　The Draft House

Fair Market Value: $ 150

Starting Bid $	Name	Phone	Bidder Number	Email
Minimum Raise $				

As you create this type of bid sheet, you will need to determine the minimum bid increment or raise and the starting bid. There really is no rule of thumb here. One approach is to look at the fair market value of the item and start the bidding at half its value. The minimum bid increment or raise is the amount that each person must bid over and above the previous bidder. A five dollar increment is a good place to start for items under $50. Ten dollars works well for items between $50 and $150. Incremental amounts for items over $150 could be $20 to $25. Regardless of your approach here, "consider your audience" and adjust accordingly.

There are two schools of thought regarding the management of bid sheets if you are not using software. One is that the bid sheets can be professionally printed in duplicate with one copy staying with the item and the other going to the check out area. If you choose this option, be sure to budget for the added expense or get a printer that will donate the form production as their contribution. The other approach is to have one copy of the bid sheet and the item together but they MUST be tagged with the proper item number. The goal here is for the check-out workers to be able to easily identify the correct item for the winner.

Buy It Now

EBay has influenced us in many ways. The BUY IT NOW option gives the decisive bidder a chance to do an end-run on the whole thing and snap up an item they want without competing or waiting. The price should be near the maximum that you might expect in a competitive bid. This practice is often done on items that are extremely popular and will bring a good price.

For example, let's say that a Weekend Getaway at a Beach House is up for bid. The fair market value is $950, the starting bid is $250 and the minimum raise is $50. The "Buy It Now" price could be placed at $750. The bidder that selects this option ensures that he or she wins the item and still pays less than fair market value.

There are a few other things to consider as you plan your bidding process. First of all, some bidders do not follow the requirements for raising a bid even though the minimum raise is listed on the bid sheet. Most of the time, this is not done intentionally. Or, at least the charitable part of us likes to THINK it isn't intentional. As a result, you will need to set policy guidelines regarding this situation. To do this, ask yourself these questions:

- How should your monitors handle bids that do not meet the minimum raise requirements?

- Will you disqualify the highest bid if the minimum raise requirement was not met?

This may seem a bit trivial, but if you don't plan your policy ahead of time, chaos can occur and guests involved in the process are left with a bad experience. We recommend that you keep enough monitors in the Silent Auction area to observe bidders. Should they find that someone has not met the minimum raise requirement, they can speak to the guest and change the bid prior to someone else bidding. It's best to stick to the rules of the bidding process to avoid negative outcomes.

Second, how do you handle a high bid when you can not decipher the person's name? It is very difficult to award the winner if you don't know who it is. One way to solve the problem is to ask people to print their information (and hope you can read THAT). Complete the first line of the bid sheet as a sample for the bidders to follow. If you find that you still can not decipher someone's writing, you may want to make an announcement and ask that individuals who have been bidding on the item find the monitor responsible for the item to verify their bids. Set a time limit though. Reward the folks who didn't make your job impossible. Move to the next bid on the list if you can't make out the winner because they just wouldn't work with you.

Third, occasionally an item is so popular that the donor decides to double the donation. For example, let's say that a camping trip with the football coach is really causing some excitement. The coach decides that rather than do just one campout, he will do two. Be prepared with a plan to handle this **wonderful** situation. You may have blank bid sheets that you can use to write up another or you may choose to take the top highest bidders. The fair thing to do here is to have everyone pay the same. If the last bid was $200 and the next to last was $175 – ask the second place person if they want to match it to get their own trip. Bet they will if you ask nicely!

Regardless of your approach to solving these issues, it is very important to have a game plan in place and to make sure that all of your Silent Auction monitors understand and enforce the rules.

Prepare Item Descriptions

Each item or package in the silent auction must have a description sheet displayed at the silent auction tables. There are two objectives here. You want to catch the attention of the bidders (usually done through the name of the item), and you want to provide detailed information so that the bidders know exactly what they are purchasing.

The description sheet can be printed on brightly colored paper or stationery to enhance its appearance. It's not necessary for all of them to be exactly alike. Actually, its more interesting, it easy to do, and it has great eye appeal if they are all different... but READABLE.

Make certain that all dates, if applicable, are accurate. Include the calendar date and the day of the week. Expiration dates are also extremely important.

Any restrictions regarding the use of the item should also be included. For example, owners of a lake house may not want pets in their home. Other restrictions could be that a dining gift certificate is only valid on a Sunday – in August – with a full moon – if you wear blue.

Silent Auction goers bid on items that "tickle their fancy." The written description of the item needs to be colorful and fun. Let's say that you are auctioning a beach retreat weekend for girls.

> Spend a relaxing weekend with the girls working on your tan,
> sleeping in, and enjoying hours of girl talk!
>
> This gorgeous weekend get-away home sleeps 12,
> and sits *right on the beach*!

The title of this item could be something fun like "Babes Beach Blanket Bingo".

As you read this did you get the desire to win this get-away? When people read something that piques their interest – they'll bid, and bid, and bid!

Remember to be creative and have fun with your descriptions. Enlist the helpful minds of other folks. This could be a good luncheon topic.

Gift Certificates

Some of your donations will not be tangible items that can be taken home. The weekend get-away is a perfect example. You want each winner to have something to take home with them as a reminder of the item. Creating gift certificates is the best way to go.

Gift certificates for services, meals, etc. are popular. Because they are equal to cash, it's best to place the gift certificate in a labeled envelope and keep it at the check-out table or auction pick-up area sorted by item number.

Set Up the Silent Auction Display

Just as important as the name and description of each donation is the display. The display should include the item, associated enhancements (also known as props) to help sell the item, pencils, the bid sheet, and item description.

As you plan for the silent auction area, use the theme of the event as your guide for decorations. If you are using blue tablecloths, stars, and balloons that should be evident throughout the venue.

Arrange description sheets next to each item or package. One idea is to use brightly colored gift bags with tissue that match your colors and theme, and place the descriptions on them. When used consistently, this approach will give the auction goers a focal point to look for the description. Another idea is to use clear, acrylic 8 1/2" x 11" frames to hold description sheets. Use your imagination!

Make sure the description pages are easy to read and standing close to the item vs. lying down flat on the table. When your bidders walk into the silent auction area, they will be able to quickly identify the description of each item.

Props are used to enhance the appeal of the item. For example if there is a sailboat donated you could use a skipper's hat and a life preserver to showcase it. This is extremely important for items that are paper related such as gift certificates and items that are too large to adequately display. In some instances, these enhancements may be part of the item. The best way to get props is to make a list of what you think you might need and distribute it to all the committee members.

Here are some fun prop ideas:

- Dinner Gift Certificate – use a napkin in a napkin ring sitting on a plate

- Salons and Spas –How about a loofah sponge and some body lotion?

- Dinner Party – Ask the donor to prepare a dessert as the prop and the winner can take the dessert home!

- Happy Hour – A wine glass, some real or artificial grapes, a cheese board and a bottle of aspirin is fun!

- Trips – Use souvenirs or travel posters of the location. You may want to put it all in a suitcase if you have plenty of room.

- Event Tickets – Typically you can get promotional posters for the event at no cost! You may want to collect easels to display these so that they are easily seen.

If you choose to add the Wish List option, create a separate area that is devoted SPECIFICALLY to that opportunity. Use props that represent the items on your list.

Opening and Monitoring the Auction

Typically the silent auction is open at the beginning of the event and guests can begin shopping and bidding once they check in. Auction monitors should be stationed in the silent auction area to assist guests with any questions. In addition, these monitors provide security and manage bid sheet activity. Some items will be so popular that the bid sheet may become full. Supply your monitors with additional bid sheets and instruct them to attach the new bid sheet on top of the original so that bidders can track their progress. We had one case where the bid sheet mysteriously vanished and then re-appeared moments before the close of the auction. That kid REALLY wanted that puppy. Be prepared to replace purloined bid sheets to head off this temptation to larceny.

Some of your monitors could model expensive jewelry or any other items that you may not want to display. Monitors should also watch for items that aren't being bid on. You may decide to reduce the minimum bids to get the bidding started on an item, or bundle a couple of slow items into a "package deal."

The silent auction stays open the majority of the evening. This allows plenty of time for folks to bid.

Closing the Auction

Prior to the event, determine the best approach for bid sheet and item pickup. There are a couple of ways to manage this process. You may choose to have your monitors pick up the bid sheets along with the item and take them to the check out area, or you may simply pick up the bid sheets and leave the items in the room if it can be secured. If you choose the latter, be prepared for two lines – one for check out payment and one for item pick up. In this scenario, volunteers stay with the items and retrieve them for guests when presented with a paid receipt. Neither of these approaches is necessarily better than another. Select the best for your floor plan.

Set the closing time of the auction approximately one hour prior to the end of the evening. For example, if the event is scheduled from 7:00pm to 10:00pm, close the auction at 9:00pm. Print the closing time for the silent auction in the program.

It's a good idea to close the auction by sections. For example, the gift basket zone could be closed first and then 15 minutes later another. The best way to approach this is to close one-fourth of the items every 15 minutes. This creates urgency. People can continue to shop in the other zones while you are getting the check out area organized.

Emphasize to your monitors that bid sheets should be picked up quickly. Even the most honest person will get caught up in the excitement of winning an item. They may even feel tempted to sign their name after the "bell has rung." A rapid retrieval of bid sheets helps to keep people honest.

Note: Check-out will not begin until all bid sheets are collected.

Announce the closing of each zone. Use a microphone, if available, or a noisemaker. Feel free to be creative here. Use your theme as your guide.

Organization is the key to a successful check-out process. Regardless of where the items are placed for pick up, keep them in numerical order.

Silent Auction Check-out

Guests should already know where, when and how to check-out. Communicate all of this at check-in time and post a few signs with the information as well.

The check out process leaves a lasting impression on your guests. It literally can make or break the event. The inconvenience of waiting in long lines to pay is typically the biggest problem. To avoid this issue, make sure you have plenty of volunteers whose drink of choice for the evening are non-alcoholic beverages. This ensures accuracy and clear thinking.

Would you be surprised to learn that we think the check-out process is much easier when you use auction software? Well, it is. Consider using it here, even if you don't see its value anywhere else in the process. Auction software is designed to facilitate a fast and efficient check-out resulting in happy guests who look forward to next year's event… and happy volunteers who aren't making "late night" mistakes that cost time and maybe revenue!

The check-out area should be away from the main party. If you are doing your check-out without auction software, the following process works best.

Bid Sheet Organization

Organize bid sheets alphabetically as they are collected at the check out table. Prepare an alphabetical sorting system prior to the evening so that the volunteers know exactly where to put the bid sheets. As the bid sheets arrive, alphabetize them by the last name of the winner. This way, when the winner arrives to pay, all of their bid sheets can be located under their name.

The simplest way to let guests know if they've won an item is to post a winner list conspicuously away from the check out tables. You don't want non-winners to have to stand in a line to find out that they didn't win.

Payment

After all the bid sheets are collected prepare totals for each winner. If you are using auction software, you will be able to print an invoice for each winner before they can find their checkbook.

One quick way to facilitate payment is to swipe a guest's credit card when they check in. If they do not win any items, then the credit card receipt has no total and is not processed. If they do win items, you will be able to process their credit card and have it ready for them to sign when they arrive at the check-out table. The few guests who may be uncomfortable with this idea can be offered traditional payment opportunities – check and cash – or allow them to pay with a credit card at the end.

To expedite the payment process, consider forming two lines – one for the guests who have pre-swiped credit cards and those choosing traditional forms of payment.

After you have received payment, give each winner a paid receipt with the item numbers on it. Then instruct them to take the receipt to the item pick-up area.

Item pick-up will need several people who will deliver the items to the guests. You don't want to let guests wander in and help themselves.

Check-Out Documentation

It is important to note the winning amount of each auction item and the name of the person who won it. Have someone at the check-out table enter the information onto a spreadsheet. If it is not possible to enter it into a computer at this time, keep track of it so that it can be entered later.

Final Check-Out Procedures

- Identify items that have not been paid for or picked up.
  - Attach the bid sheets to them,
  - make a list of them,
  - give the list and items to the Silent Auction Chairperson.
  - Prepare a report indicating the total collected and outstanding payments due for the Silent Auction Chairperson.
- Give the treasurer the cash, checks and credit card receipts.

Documentation

Good documentation is critical to a successful silent auction. Throughout this book we've discussed the information that you will need to put into a database. Initially, documentation is done as you collect donor forms – each item is logged onto a spreadsheet and assigned a category. The second phase is done when items are collected. At this point you'll be assigning numbers to each. The remaining documentation occurs during and after the auction.

After the auction, you'll want to analyze your data so that you can use it in the planning for the next year's event. Typically, you'll want to identify the following:

- Items that brought in the most money
- Highest bidders

This information will help guide your planning for next year's event.

Chapter 15

What am I bid for this JOB!!!

The Live Auction

The live auction is an opportunity to generate a lot of money for your organization. The keys to your success are:

- a great auctioneer
- getting terrific items to auction
- generating a lot of interest in the items prior to and during the event
- timing of the live auction during the event

Let's look at each of these concepts:

A Great Auctioneer

The auctioneer is critical to the success of your live auction. He or she should have good experience and have excellent references. A great auctioneer will be able to engage the audience and motivate them to bid. If you hire an auctioneer outside of your organization, make sure to have additional people on the platform who know many of the attendees and have good personalities. They identify and encourage potential bidders (perhaps by name and with threats of blackmail or other enticements) while the auctioneer does his/her job.

So how do you find this person? You may be fortunate to have someone in your organization who is a professional auctioneer, but in the event that you don't, do some research. Check with other organizations to get names to contact. Another source is to read auction notices in the newspaper and look at the contact information for the auctioneer. There is also a national association of auctioneers that can be accessed via the Internet. Check our website for a link -

www.storymasterpress.com/auctionhelp

Typically when you hire an auctioneer, you will sign a contract. Before you do, you will want to weigh several factors carefully. Price should not be the only determining factor in making your decision. You should also consider:

- **Auctioneer Specialty and Experience.** Many auctioneers specialize in only a few types of auctions. Ask about his/her specialty and the number of auctions they typically do in a year. You want to make sure that the auctioneer has experience in auctioning the type of merchandise you have.

- **Referrals.** Auctioneers have plenty of success stories to share. Get a list of their clients. Call some and ask them for their thoughts.

- **Licensing.** This may not be a requirement for your auctioneer, but auctioneers who hold licenses have met scholastic and accreditation requirements. They may also be a little more expensive.

- **Professional Affiliation.** Members of the National Auctioneers Association are governed by a Code of Ethics, which ensures professionalism.

- **Reputation.** An auctioneer's reputation is critical to the success of an auction. Their reputation is a blend of experience and character. An auctioneer who is trusted and respected in your community will be a success with your guests.

You may be tempted to ask a celebrity to be your auctioneer in an effort to draw a crowd. A word of caution here - unless the celebrity has excellent auctioning experience, you may want to reconsider. It is better to have someone experienced in auctioning rather than someone famous who can't produce results. Auction fever isn't automatic. It is CREATED by a talented auctioneer.

Getting Terrific Items to Auction

Typically, items of high value are the best to auction to a live audience because they tend to generate a lot of interest and bidding activity. Here are some examples:

- Handmade projects by groups (i.e. classes, teachers, choir, band)
- Trips with airfare and lodging
- Expensive art and jewelry
- Vacation homes
- AKA registered puppies
- Group activities with favorite people (i.e. minister, principal, teachers, etc.) (Sell it twice)

As you do your planning, list the types of items that you'd like to have in the live auction. This will give your volunteers direction as they begin soliciting donations.

Generating Interest in Items Prior to and During the Event

People bid on items that they want… and that OTHERS want! You want to make sure that the items are publicized prior to the event. Use every opportunity to describe the items that have been donated. Consider putting a list in an article and place it in your organizations newsletter. Include pictures whenever you can.

Create a viewing area at the event venue that is easily accessible and noticeable. Ask the check-in volunteers to encourage guests to spend time looking at the items that will be up for bid during the live auction. Just as in the silent auction, use props to add interest to the items.

Timing of the Auction

The timing of the live auction should be well thought out and positioned so that you monopolize the guests attention. To be successful, the auctioneer needs to have everyone's attention. Consider having the live auction after a seated dinner or perhaps during dessert. Basically, it should be held mid-evening.

The rule of thumb here is to give folks plenty of time to enjoy the party and bid on items in the silent auction prior to the live auction. You may want to consider having the silent auction close after the live auction so that if they don't win anything in the live auction, they still have a chance in the silent auction.

Auction Organization

Now that we've discussed these critical areas, let's turn our attention to the organization of the auction. Each guest should be given a numbered auction paddle at check in. An auction paddle is used when people are bidding. They hold it in the air to place their bid. A paddle can be a large piece of paper, colored construction paper, or an actual auction paddle on a stick. You could use your theme to come up with interesting shapes and sizes. The most important thing to consider is that it needs to be seen well when held in the air.

Assign volunteers to fill the role of auction spotters. Typically one spotter to every 40 bidders works well. These folks watch the crowd and help the auctioneer identify the bidders as they raise their paddles. As a guest raises his paddle, a spotter should go and stand by that bidder to help the auctioneer find them in the crowd.

Once the bidding stops and the auctioneer calls the winner, the paddle number should be noted next to the item along with the final bid. Assign this responsibility to a live auction volunteer. If you are not using auction software to generate your forms, this format works well.

Live Auction Bid Sheet			
Item Number	Item Description	Bidder Number	Bid Amount

Prior to the live auction, list the item numbers and descriptions on the form in the order in which they will be auctioned. This will help the process move quicker and ensure that it is accurate.

178 Ruth McCurdy & Linda Oppenheim

The Big Board

Live auction oftentimes include a "Big Board." The big board is a "warm up" for the live auction and is open for a specified short period of time such as 15 to 20 minutes. It is used for items that have the potential to bring more money when talked about and shown. These items could include a diamond necklace, excellent seats at a sporting event, an opportunity to ride in a rodeo parade, private television station tour, etc. Your best bet is to have four to six items total.

This board is located in the live auction area. Generally, several people are responsible for manning the Big Board. Their responsibilities include generating interest in the items on the Big Board and getting bids from the crowd. You'll want to make sure that you recruit enthusiastic, outgoing people who are not afraid to catch your guests' interest for this job. This is how it works:

A big dry-erase board is divided into sections. Each section has the name of an item in it. The announcers describe each item as they start the bid. The announcer establishes the beginning bid and asks people in the crowd to raise it. After it is raised, that number is recorded under the item and the announcer moves to the next item. Once all items have been bid on, the crowd is encouraged to shout out bids for items that they want. Each time a new bid is made, it is written under the item. To generate excitement, you can ring a bell signifying a higher bid has been called.

The Big Board looks like this:

Diamond Necklace	Razar Football Tickets	Rodeo Parade Grand Marshall
Value $ 500	Value $250	Value – Priceless!
Minimum Bid $150	Minimum Bid $75	Minimum Bid $100
Couples Day at a Spa	**Weekend Getaway**	**Pearl Earrings**
Value $650	Value $450	Value $300
Minimum Bid $175	Minimum Bid $125	Minimum Bid $100

To make this work, ask two or three volunteers to work with the announcer to spot bidders. As with any event, people will get busy talking to one another and may not focus on the bidding at this board. Have some of your volunteers walk among the crowd and encourage the guests to take a look at the Big Board and participate in the auction.

After the Big Board closes, jot down the guests bid number and the amount bid on each item and take them to the check out area. Use a form like this one:

Big Board Bid Sheet			
Item Number	**Item Description**	**Bidder Number**	**Bid Amount**

One final note about the live auction. Make sure that the ***sound system*** in your venue works well with a large crowd. Many dollars can be lost when people can't hear the auctioneer.

Chapter 16

Sure wish someone had written this all down.

The Event Notebook

As the chairperson for your fundraising event, the best legacy you can leave behind is an in-depth record of everything that was done to make your event a huge success! The most common approach to documenting the how-tos and results is to create a notebook. This may seem to be an overwhelming task, but we took care of that for you by adding a bullet to each of your committee chairpersons' job descriptions indicating their responsibility in developing their respective notes for the book.

To assist your committee chairpersons with the development of their notes, we have developed a format they can follow. This format can be downloaded free at www.storymasterpress.com/auctionhelp.

- committee name
- committee person's name
- committee members
- committee activities (include what you did and how it was accomplished)
- things that worked well
- things we would do differently next time
- associated costs
- forms/letters/software used: (include printed forms and CD-Rom or diskette with forms)

These topics are universal across all committees; however, there are specific details you'll want to capture on some of the committees. They are listed below:

Invitations and Reservations Committee

- actual invitation and reservation card
- mailing list
- number of invitations sent and number of attendees
- list of people/businesses who bought tables

Program Advertising Committee

- Sample ads and costs per ads
- List of ad patrons with contact information
- Ad patron thank-you letter

Underwriter Solicitation Committee

- List of underwriters with contact information
- Underwriter letter
- Underwriter thank-you letter

Publicity Committee

- copies of articles used in publicity
- publicity posters
- flyers

Program Committee

a printed program

Group Project/Donations Committee

- list of donations/projects and donors
- pictures of the donations

Live Auction Committee
- donations and donors spreadsheet
- donor solicitation worksheet
- final tally on money raised during live auction
- auctioneer contract (if used)
- list of big spenders

Silent Auction Committee
- donations and donors spreadsheet
- donor solicitation worksheet
- final tally on money raised during silent auction
- list of big spenders
- picture of Silent Auction set-up

Auction Check-In and Reception Committee
names of guests who attended the event

Auction Check-Out Committee
list of items, guests who purchased them and the final bid for each

Treasurer
- budget
- profit and loss statement for the event
- copies of checks and deposit slips
- copies of invoices and receipts

As the Event Chairperson, you really are a committee of one so here is what you need to place in the notebook:

- event timeline
- the theme of the event
- volunteer recruiting materials
- committee meeting agendas
- any written policies or procedures
- all venue documentation – menu, floor plans, contracts, etc.
- things that worked well
- things we would do differently next time
- associated costs
- forms/letters/software used: (include printed forms and CD-Rom or diskette with forms)

Now how do you assemble all of this? Get a three-ring, view binder, dividers, and plastic sheet protectors. Make the cover page for the notebook and put it in the clear pocket on the front of the binder. Next, put each committee's notes in a section with their name and use the plastic sheet protectors for items like the invitation, program, etc. Finally, make your table of contents by listing the name of the committees and the associated chapter numbers.

Creating the event notebook isn't difficult, it is just a little time consuming. We recommend that you give your committee chairpersons a deadline for submitting their notes. The deadline should be set within two weeks after the event while the enthusiasm is high and the memories are fresh.

Whew! You made it! Congratulations on a great job! Check with your organization to see where they want the notebook kept until the next event and place it there for safekeeping.

Perspective and Attitude

Chapter 17

ABC's for a Successful Auction Chairperson

A – Ask for volunteers – most people are willing to help if they feel needed.

B – Brainstorm ideas about everything. Involve as many people as possible in idea-sharing.

C – Communicate clearly and often.

D – Delegate responsibilities to your volunteers and then let go!

E – Excitement about the event is contagious! Share yours with everyone!

F – Find ways to make the process fun. People don't mind putting a lot of effort into something when they are having a good time together.

G – Generate interest in the event by telling everyone you know about it.

H – Honor your volunteers' time. Remember that they, as well as you, have other commitments.

I – Invite newcomers to the process. Take advantage of fresh ideas.

J – Jumpstart your event with a kick-off meeting that energizes the group.

K – Knowledge is power. Keep track of everything that is done throughout the event so that it can be used in planning future events.

L – Look for opportunities to learn from others. Touch base with previous chairpersons for the event and build on their ideas.

M – Motivate your volunteers throughout the process. Make certain they have what they need from you and feel appreciated.

N – Nuances make the difference in meeting or exceeding your guests' expectations. Focus on details.

O – Organize your time wisely. Make sure to carve out some time for yourself!

P – Publicize the event at every opportunity. Don't assume that everyone knows about it!

Q – Quickly respond to your volunteers needs. This ensures that they will be able to accomplish their assigned tasks in a timely manner.

R – Recognize your volunteers' efforts on a regular basis. Use email or a newsletter to mention who they are and what they are doing! People love to see their names in print!

S – Set goals that are high and achievable.

T – Track your progress along the way and keep your volunteers and the organization posted. Celebrate milestones that you reach.

U – Utilize an automated database to house all of your information.

V – Value your volunteers.

W – Write thank you notes to all volunteers when the event is over.

X – eXpect results from your committee members. Hold them accountable for completing their assigned tasks.

Y – You are in charge but not a dictator. When problems occur, involve others in solving them.

Z – Zero-in on all of your activities and prioritize them when you feel a little overwhelmed.

INDEX

publicity, 15, 16, 17, 22, 60, 61, 65,
 67, 90, 101, 102, 103, 104, 105,
 118, 129, 159, 182
Publicity, 43, 53, 60, 61, 101, 103,
 126, 137, 156, 159, 182

R

Reception, 53, 68, 69, 75, 183
Reservations, 33, 53, 72, 73, 75, 129,
 137, 138, 144, 150, 182
Rules, 143, 144, 145

S

silent auction, 10, 16, 17, 19, 22, 23,
 25, 26, 29, 31, 53, 67, 96, 127,
 145, 156, 157, 160, 165, 167, 168,
 169, 172, 175, 183

T

thank-you, 15, 17, 26, 49, 54, 80, 81,
 90, 91, 107, 127, 128, 143
Theme, 95, 98, 132

treasurer, 15, 17, 55, 57, 61, 63, 65,
 67, 172

U

underwriting, 31, 56, 57, 92, 118, 120
Underwriting, 33, 93, 118, 119

V

venue, 9, 10, 14, 17, 19, 21, 22, 23,
 24, 55, 67, 69, 71, 76, 77, 79, 88,
 96, 105, 114, 129, 131, 153, 167,
 175, 179, 184
Venue, 19, 24, 91, 93
venues, 20, 21
volunteer, 5, 8, 14, 15, 26, 35, 37, 39,
 40, 43, 44, 45, 48, 50, 51, 54, 55,
 76, 88, 105, 111, 112, 113, 145,
 176, 184, 188
Volunteer, 35, 36, 43, 46, 47, 48